Elizabeth Dwight

Manifesting His Beauty and Displaying His Worth

With Cords of Love

The Memoirs of Elizabeth Dwight
Missionary Wife and Mother

Compiled by Harrison Dwight
Edited by Jennifer Adams

With Cords of Love: The Memoirs of Elizabeth Dwight, Missionary Wife and Mother

is taken from

A Memoir of Mrs. Elizabeth Dwight
By Rev. Harrison G.O. Dwight
M.W. Dodd, Brick Church Chapel: New York, 1840

This grammatically revised edition with
additional material is published by

🏛 CORNER PILLAR PRESS
"Let our daughters be as corner pillars,
Fashioned as for a palace."
Psalm 144:12

Copyright © 2012 Jennifer Adams
Forest, VA
Printed in the United States of America

ISBN: 978-0-9844320-6-6

cornerpillarpress@gmail.com
www.cornerpillarpress.com

Front Cover: Mrs. Elizabeth Dwight

This Book is Affectionately Dedicated to
My Lovely Daughters

Mary Bethany
Elisabeth Victoria
Sarah Kate
Anna Grace

May we worship the Lord Jesus
together, forever in heaven;
May you be my glory and my joy
and my crown of exultation
before the Lord at His coming.

And to *Elisabeth* in particular:
May the Lord bless you as a mother,
Giving you a son like John the Baptist,
Who will prepare the way for the Lord.

Contents

Preface to the Series

With Cords of Love: The Memoirs of Elizabeth Dwight, Missionary Wife and Mother is the sixth book in the "Completer to a Contender for the Faith" series.[1] These books are published to cast a vision for our daughters of godliness, faithfulness, and biblical femininity. Each of these books focuses on a woman in history who has impacted the world for Christ, with a special emphasis on her role as a completer to a "contender for the faith." This phrase comes from Jude 1:3 which says, "I felt the necessity to write to you appealing that you *contend earnestly for the faith* which was once for all delivered to the saints." Throughout church history, God has raised up men to contend for the truth of the gospel. The faithfulness of their wives to encourage them to "fight the good fight"[2] and "finish the course"[3] is worth studying and imitating.

In the "Completer to a Contender for the Faith" series, we seek to publish the original writings of such women or any other first-hand material concerning them. It is no exaggeration to say that many of the men whom God has used throughout church history have fulfilled their ministry, in large part, due to the prayers, encouragement, and sacrifice of their wives. Without this important but often unseen ministry, the church today may not be standing quite as high on the shoulders of those who have gone before.

---

[1] The other books are *A Basket of Summer Fruit,* by Susannah Spurgeon; *In Love with Christ: The Narrative of Sarah Edwards,* by Sarah Edwards; *Ann Judson: Missionary Wife*, by Arabella Stuart—revised, edited, and expanded by Jennifer Adams; *Delighting in Her Heavenly Bridegroom: The Memoirs of Harriet Newell, Teenage Missionary Wife* edited and annotated by Jennifer Adams; and *Following Her Beloved: The Memoirs of Henrietta Shuck, Missionary Wife and Mother,* compiled by Jeremiah Jeter, edited and expanded by Jennifer Adams.
[2] II Timothy 4:7
[3] Ibid.

There are several predominant themes that run parallel in the lives of these women: 1) they each had their own relationship with Christ, independent of their husbands, from which they drew their strength; 2) they were intellectually strong, theologically like-minded, and of a kindred spirit with their husbands; 3) they shared a sweet spiritual union with their husbands that fortified their men to face the meanest foe and graced them to enjoy God's presence together before the throne in a way that they never could alone; 4) they believed one of the best ways that they could serve God was to allow Him to cut and fashion them into the "velvet steel" upon which their husbands could lean; 5) they embraced their husbands' vision and ministry fully, and gave of themselves not only to their husbands and children, but also to the church and the spread of the gospel; 6) there came a point in their husbands' lives when they faced large-scale persecution due to contending for the faith. These women joined their husbands in "not [being] ashamed of the gospel"[4] by partaking in "the fellowship of His sufferings."[5] As a result, the gospel advanced through their husbands' ministries, across international borders, and down through the generations—even to this day.

These women were not perfect. They had struggles and weaknesses—but they each counted Christ and His gospel worthy of their lives. For this reason, they go down in history as women whom we want to emulate. Our prayer is that as we study the lives of these women, our daughters will embrace a vision for the ministry of being a "completer to a contender for the faith." Furthermore, we pray that our daughters will be pointed to the fountainhead of love and strength from which these women drew—the Lord Jesus Christ.

---

[4] Romans 1:16
[5] Philippians 3:10

Editor's Preface

With Cords of Love: The Memoirs of Elizabeth Dwight, Missionary Wife and Mother is the original edition of Elizabeth's memoirs with grammatical and stylistic revisions. Formal titles and surnames have been replaced with primary names. Scripture and hymn references have been footnoted. Chapter divisions and titles have been added. The layout of the material has been slightly rearranged. Portions of letters with extensive detail regarding Turkish climate, culture, and custom have been omitted. The work has been bathed in prayer. Special thanks to Mary Bethany Adams, Bethany Joshua, and Courtney Joshua for razor-sharp proofreading!

With Cords of Love: The Memoirs of Elizabeth Dwight, Missionary Wife and Mother is the sixth book in the Completer to a Contender for the Faith Series. The first two books, *A Basket of Summer Fruit* by Susannah Spurgeon and *In Love with Christ: The Narrative of Sarah Edwards* give a glimpse into the heart and life of a pastor's wife. The accounts of these women exude the love of Christ as they detail the unsearchable riches of His grace and model biblical womanhood in supporting their husbands' ministries. The second two books, *Ann Judson: Missionary Wife* and *Delighting in Her Heavenly Bridegroom: The Memoirs of Harriet Newell, Teenage Missionary Wife* magnify the worth of Christ in suffering and dying for Him in missions. The accounts of these women emanate the sweet aroma of their sacrifice as they gave their lives to accompany their husbands in the spread of the gospel among the nations. The last two books, *Following Her Beloved: The Memoirs of Henrietta Shuck, Missionary Wife and Mother* and *With Cords of Love: The Memoirs of Elizabeth Dwight, Missionary Wife and Mother* depict the love and labor of a missionary wife and mother. The accounts of these women model biblical womanhood in and through the home and demonstrate how to persevere in hard circumstances by clinging to the love of God in Christ crucified. While there are numerous accounts of nineteenth century missionary wives, there are not many who were conscientious of their God-given ministry to raise their children for the Lord. Elizabeth Dwight stands out as a shining example of a faithful missionary wife and mother who rightly understood her primary ministry to her children—and who by God's grace—sacrificed, labored, and prayed to fulfill it that she might manifest Christ's beauty and display His worth.

Editor's Introduction

America's first missionary wives suffered incalculably for the sake of the gospel—they endured illness and deprivation, war and separation, the death of their beloved children and the loss of their own lives. They manifested Christ's beauty and displayed His worth by trading their earthly treasures for heavenly ones. The fragrance of their sacrifice perpetually rises before the throne while lingering still on earth, enticing others to follow.

The faithfulness of these women deserves to be memorialized in every heart, allowing them to "still speak"[6] of the worth of Christ in suffering and dying for Him in missions. However, there is another kind of woman worth studying and imitating— the woman who models on the mission field how to be a godly wife and mother. The missionary wife has the challenge of raising her children to be lights in the midst of the very "crooked and perverse generation" that she and her husband are trying to reach.[7] The spiritual warfare in such an undertaking is fierce. Like Nehemiah, missionary parents often find themselves building their homes with one hand and wielding the sword with the other. It does not take long before they get wounded in the fight—yet they must press on.[8] It is often in their weakness that God reveals His strength.[9] Their perseverance in spite of their scars magnifies Christ's beauty and displays His worth. Elizabeth Dwight is an example of such a woman.

Elizabeth and her husband, Harrison, were among America's first missionaries to Turkey.[10] Elizabeth gave birth to four sons on the mission field. She was a faithful wife and mother whose

---

[6] Hebrews 11:4

[7] Philippians 2:15

[8] Philippians 3:14

[9] II Corinthians 12:9

[10] They set sail for Malta in 1830, and then two years later, settled in Constantinople, Turkey.

chief desire was to see her children come to faith in Christ. She wrote:

> "My children must be converted early in life" is a sentiment which ought to be adopted by every Christian mother and deserves to be written in letters of gold daily before her eyes; or rather, so indelibly printed upon the heart as never, for one hour, to be forgotten. . . . True, it must be accomplished through the grace of God, to quote your own language, "how freely bestowed!"

She sacrificed, labored, and prayed toward this end, with the vision that their conversion would lead to an increase in laborers on the mission field. However, not long after arriving on the mission field, Elizabeth experienced physical complications that left her incapacitated. When unable to rise, she attempted to train her children from bed. In spite of her best efforts, she was constantly concerned for their souls. She confided her feelings of failure to a close friend:

> Oh, my dear children! Oh, my unfaithfulness and neglect towards them! What will become of them? Where would they go if God should call them away now? Could I die in peace feeling that my duty has thus far been faithfully discharged towards them? These thoughts are passing through my mind from day to day, and from morning light to evening shade; and yet it seems to me that I am dull and do not feel, in any measure, as mothers in America do, and as every mother is under the most solemn obligations to feel.

Her husband commented on the above letter:

> This was written by one who was eminently devoted to the education of her children and who faithfully and perseveringly aimed to bring all her instructions to bear upon the salvation of their souls. Even when in severe bodily pain, and with her strength prostrated by her truly discouraging disease, she often gathered her children around her and manifested the greatest delight in their instruction. Her patience in bearing with their inattention at such times of weakness, and her perseverance in endeavoring to excite their interest in instruction when from the state of her body haste and peevishness would almost have been pardonable, were truly surprising.

Elizabeth agonized over how her physical limitations affected her children, but she did not give in to despair. She learned to rebuke feelings of failure and replace them with faith in God's promises.

Faith in God's Promises

The cost of being a missionary is often most keenly felt by the wife and mother whose primary domain is the home—for it is the comforts of home that must be left for the sake of gospel. The pastor who preached the memorial sermon for the proto-martyr of modern missions, Harriet Newell, said of missionary wives:

> The wife of a missionary, when influenced by the Spirit of Christ, gives still more remarkable evidence of self-denial and devotion—evidence, I say, more remarkable because for her to forsake friends and country is an instance of greater self-denial. The tie which binds her to her relatives and her home is stronger. Her mind is more delicate in its construction and

more sensible to the tenderness of natural relations and the delights of domestic life. When, therefore, she forsakes all for the name of Christ, she makes a higher effort—she offers a more costly sacrifice, and thus furnishes a more conspicuous proof that her love of Christ transcends all earthly affection.[11]

Why would a wife and mother leave the comforts of home to accompany her husband on the mission field? It is for the sake of the Lamb and the glory of His name. His worth is displayed through the lives of those who willingly sacrifice for the furtherance of His gospel.

While Elizabeth esteemed Christ as worthy of her life, she was deeply concerned how the idolatrous culture of the mission field might affect her children, and she grieved for the lack of the spiritual privileges they suffered by not living in a Christian country. She wrote, "What will become of our little ones is a question that arises in our hearts daily and causes no little solicitude." In another letter she explained:

> You can have no idea, my dear friend, what an anxiety it is to Christian parents in these countries to train up a family of children amidst such follies and wickedness—to hear them ask what means this, and why is that, and at the same time to have no churches to lead them to but such as are polluted with idolatry.

Although Elizabeth's concerns were real, she learned to replace anxiety for her children with faith in God's promises, remembering that salvation is a work of the Lord,[12] and that it takes just as much grace to convert a child in America as it does anywhere. She wrote:

---

[11] *Delighting in Her Heavenly Bridegroom: The Memoirs of Harriet Newell, Teenage Missionary Wife* (Forest, VA: Corner Pillar Press, 2011) 248.
[12] Jonah 2:9

Yet it is as easy for the Spirit of God to guide the infant heart in the ways of holiness here as anywhere, and for our consolation He has bid us to trust Him with all our concerns.[13] It is only the want of active faith that ever leads us to indulge in distressing fears.

Elizabeth recognized that she must entrust her soul and the souls of her little ones to the Lord, "who loved her and delivered Himself up for her,"[14] believing that He was working for her good.[15] She strengthened herself with the promise that the children of believers are sanctified;[16] meaning that through their parents, they are recipients of the means of grace[17] which are able to give them the wisdom that leads to salvation.[18] She cherished the promises given to believers with regard to their children:

They shall be My people and I will be their God; and I will give them one heart and one way that they may fear Me always, for their own good, and for the good of their children after them.[19]

All your sons will be taught of the Lord; and the well-being of your sons will be great.[20]

The children of Thy servants will continue, and their descendents will be established before Thee.[21]

---

[13] I Peter 5:7
[14] Galatians 2:20
[15] Romans 8:28
[16] I Corinthians 7:14
[17] i.e., recipients of the gospel, prayer, discipline, instruction in the Word, partaking in the meeting of the saints, etc.
[18] II Timothy 3:15
[19] Jeremiah 32:38-39
[20] Isaiah 54:13
[21] Psalm 102:28

Like a shepherd He will tend His flock. In His arm He will gather the lambs and carry them in His bosom; He will gently lead the nursing ewes.[22]

She recognized the need to rebuke her fears and focus on the goodness of God and the certainty of His Word. She wrote:

Dark as midnight, indeed, would be our prospects in regard to the welfare of our dear children if the promises of God were not as many and as rich for us as for you, which after all, are the main springs of hope and consolation. O for a strong and vigorous faith to seize hold of them and have our little ones now sealed the heirs of grace! Then could we contemplate with composure the storms of sorrow and temptation that may assail their path through the short journey of life and anticipate a happy meeting on the everlasting hills of light, to exclaim before our Redeemer, "Here I am and the children Thou hast given me."[23]

When meditating on God's promises, her faith was strengthened and her heart renewed, trusting that her labor in the Lord was not in vain.[24] Believing that God would make effectual the means of grace in the lives of her children, she wrote:

We are warranted from the Scriptures to expect the early conversion of our children in connection with a *faithful fulfillment* of covenant vows.[25]

---

[22] Isaiah 40:11—nursing ewes depict nursing mothers or mothers with small children, whom God gently leads.

[23] Hebrews 2:13

[24] I Corinthians 15:58

[25] It is possible by "covenant vows" she is referring to a commitment made at baptism/infant dedication to teach, discipline, pray for, protect, love, and lead her children to worship Christ with the saints—these are duties

In light of God's promises, she persevered. She said, "Let us labor and faint not, and pray without ceasing.[26] The promises are sure—our work will soon be done." As Elizabeth faithfully employed the means of grace in her mothering, she trusted the Lord to work through her weakness for His glory. The means of grace she employed include prayer, teaching, discipline, protection, love, and leading her children to worship Christ with the saints.

Prayer

Elizabeth labored in prayer for the salvation of her children, recognizing that God alone could change their hearts. She determined that what she could not do for them bodily, she would do for them in prayer. She wrote:

> What think you a Christian mother in this land of spiritual darkness must feel? How often must her closet testify to "groanings that cannot be uttered"[27] in behalf of her children; and her pillow be moistened with tears of grief when the world is hushed!

Not only did she labor in her closet, but she began a "Mother's Association," which was a gathering of missionary mothers who met for the specific purpose of praying for one another's children and encouraging one another in the Lord. After several prayer meetings she wrote:

> Though our families remain much as they were, and we see abundant cause for humiliation, we do feel an urgent necessity to go forward till our prayer shall be the prayer of

---

incumbent upon all parents and are means of grace for their children's salvation.

[26] I Thessalonians 5:17

[27] Romans 8:26

faith that lays hold on the everlasting promises and saves the soul!

Not much later, she began to see fruit in the lives of her children and was encouraged to continue to pray. She also requested prayer for her children from the church back home. In response to a letter from a believer in the States who promised to pray for her children, she wrote:

> It affords us incomparably more joy to know that our children have had one fervent prayer offered to heaven in their behalf than if treasures of gold had fallen to their inheritance.

Elizabeth truly desired that her children know Christ above all things and directed all of her mothering towards this end. She was determined to pray until they were brought into the fold:

> How much prayer is called for, and what moment can our hands and hearts be free, except when those dear objects of maternal solicitude are sweetly lost in slumber!

Her commitment to pray for her children's conversion reveals her dependence upon God to do the work within them. She viewed prayer as the vital link between her children and the Lord—the "maternal cord" by which her children were kept in the path of godliness. In response to the news of a young woman who fell into temptation, and whose mother was not a believer, she wrote:

> A child in imminent danger of shipwreck, and yet no *cord of maternal influence* around her heart to restrain her in the path of safety! No *secret act of faith* in a mother's heart has *linked* the footsteps of her wandering daughter to the throne of God!

As she witnessed the consequences of a prayer-less mother, Elizabeth was warned and took heed. We would all do well to imitate Elizabeth and not neglect this essential means of grace in the lives of our children!

Teaching

Elizabeth began teaching her first-born to read at age two. Her purpose, however, was not to raise a prodigy but to equip her son with the tools to know and serve God. She home-educated all of her children. While many missionary wives were sending their children away for an education, Elizabeth strongly believed in keeping them with her—both for their sake and for the sake of the ministry. She wrote:

> We need, greatly need, the assistance of pious children and youth *here*. There is abundant work for the children as well as the parents on missionary ground. They are wanted as examples of whatsoever is lovely,[28] to shine as stars in the midst of night.[29]

> The heathen want not only ministers of the Word, but pious, well-educated families in all the various departments of life to be the living, bright examples of the doctrines of Christianity.

> Should we succeed by the blessing of God on faithful and unremitting diligence in training up our families for the kingdom of heaven, we should do much to aid the missionary cause by giving the world some lovely exhibitions of piety.

Elizabeth believed that God had given her the responsibility to raise her children for Him. She made knowing Christ and His

---

[28] Philippians 4:8
[29] Philippians 2:15

Word the primary focus of her children's education. She directed all of her training to "preparing them for heaven." Her vision was to raise children who would be servants of the church. She exhorted others to do the same. She wrote:

> It is one of the most interesting features in the character of maternal societies that mothers are educating their children not only for heaven, but for the church.

> Beloved Christian mothers, here is room enough to scatter hundreds of your sons and daughters, who by bringing forth the sweet fruits of the Spirit, may make known with unostentatious but irresistible power the love of Christ and be the instruments through which God will save untold multitudes from endless perdition. Will you then train them [your children] wholly for God and give them up expressly to bear the glad tidings of salvation[30] to those who sit in darkness[31] if He shall see fit to use them?

Elizabeth believed that God has given parents the sacred duty of casting the vision for missions before their children. She warned parents to guard against cultivating an inordinate love for home, lest they be unable to leave when the call of God is upon them. She wrote:

> Why is it that comparatively so few who love the dear Savior have been willing to leave their native land and become missionaries of the cross, unless it is because the thing has never been placed before them until their habits of life were fixed? Is it because early education, which inspired the love of

---

[30] Isaiah 52:7
[31] Luke 1:79

home, had fastened a chain about them too strong to be broken by ordinary means?

As the mother of fours boys, Elizabeth did not believe it was too early to pray for helpmates. She counseled mothers to embrace a vision for raising their daughters to be missionary wives and mothers, praying that God would raise up suitable wives for her sons. She wrote:

Your daughter may hereafter be a solitary example of true female piety to multitudes in an unchristian or a heathen country. Educate her as much as possible to be everything that is amiable, worthy, and desirable as a wife. She may, at some future period, be the sole companion and helpmeet of a man of God, under labors most weighty and trials most severe. Life, under God, in some solemn hour, may hang on her skill and tenderness to sooth.

Some wondered whether it was wise to provide such a narrow education—what if our children do not become believers? How shall they make it in this world? Elizabeth responded:

A brother lately remarked in answer to the question, "How will our children hereafter be employed if they do not become pious?" that we had no right to make such a supposition—that we had given them to the Lord and ought always to feel and act in full assurance that they are His.

Elizabeth trusted that the Lord for whom they raised their children would also take care of them. Elizabeth lived and mothered in light of eternity, directing all of her efforts toward this single, most important goal—preparing her children to stand before the throne of a just and holy God.

Discipline

While Elizabeth does not speak directly to the subject of discipline, she must have been a faithful disciplinarian, as she was able to keep her young children with her during worship. She wrote:

> Our children, from the age of 14 or 15 months, have been accustomed to sit still in their little chairs during our family devotions, and William Buck, since he was 19 months old, has attended church meetings regularly without making any disturbance. The baby we keep within hearing, as the exercises are held in a part of Mr. Goodell's house. The congregation the past year has been respectable, as to numbers and characters, for this place.

Discipline is a means of grace to reprove sin and teach repentance. It is a mark of love and a sign of sonship.[32] It helps children see their sin, makes clear their condemnation, and points them to the Savior, who is Jesus Christ our Lord.

Protection

While Elizabeth's heart ached to see the people of Turkey come to know Christ, she understood the effect an ungodly culture could have on her children. She was careful to guard against ungodly influences and unequally-yoked relationships. She felt it her sacred duty to protect her children's purity of heart and to cultivate within them a desire for holiness. With one hand proclaiming the gospel and the other protecting her children, she built her home and contributed to the mission. She was careful not to leave her children unattended so that she could continually watch over their souls. She wrote:

---

[32] Hebrews 12:5-11

If she [the missionary mother] goes to the throne of grace, her children must be by her side, or her heart will be drawn away by the thoughts of their physical or moral danger. If she goes to church meetings, her children must go too; if she visits the sick or the lost, they must be of the party.

Love

Elizabeth recognized love as the key to winning her children's hearts so as to lead them to faith in Christ. She talked with them and played with them. She felt the weight of modeling biblical Christianity before them. She wrote:

A mother must be the model, and almost the only model of virtue and religion her children will have. She must be their teacher, their companion, their playmate, their nurse, and everything else.

Elizabeth viewed every act, from playing toys to teaching her children to read, as an opportunity to display the love of Christ. She utilized every means possible for their salvation. She wrote, "Is it not then of pressing importance that our children become pious in early life?"

Leading Children to Worship Christ with the Saints

Leading children to worship Christ with the saints is the culmination of the graces and the chief end of parenting. The public preaching of the Word, corporate prayer, the ordinances, and fellowship of the saints all testify to the gospel of Christ and are means of grace. Every Lord's Day is a foretaste of heaven. Parents who long for their children to join the heavenly chorus will diligently lead them to partake of this means of grace on earth.

Elizabeth faithfully led her children to worship Christ with the saints. She trained them to participate when young and viewed it as a sacred duty. She wanted them to partake of the blessings that come when Christ is corporately praised and to learn the discipline of sitting under the preaching of the Word. She wanted them to be recipients of every means of grace and prayed the Lord would make it effectual unto their salvation.

The Grace of Being Raised on the Mission Field

There is a grace which missionary children receive that many children do not—that of seeing Christ's worth displayed in the depth of their parents' love and sacrifice. They get to witness the power of the gospel transforming lives, participate in the birth of a church, behold the supernatural provision of God, and are trained by their parents for the work of the ministry. Their very upbringing is a testimony to the gospel and a grace to keep them on the straight and narrow. The spiritual privileges and blessings missionary children receive far outweigh the earthly benefits they leave behind.

Conclusion

Several months after giving birth to her fourth child, Elizabeth contracted the plague and died shortly thereafter. She left a grieving husband, a small baby, and three young sons, one of whom followed her to the grave the very next day. She counted the cost, knowing that death might be required to bring the gospel to Turkey. Before she left for the field she wrote:

> Missions is a work that has engaged the most earnest desires of my heart, and if I am not deceived, to which I would most willingly devote my strength and whatever God may have bestowed upon me; and I would hope that even life might not seem too dear a sacrifice.

> When we are led to feel that [missions] is what God commands, and when the appalling condition of the poor

perishing arises to view, and the worth of only one soul is contemplated, the thought of trials vanishes, and no sacrifice seems too great if we can but meliorate their state.

She prepared for the battle and suited up in her spiritual armor, readying herself to partake in the fellowship of Christ's sufferings.[33] She wrote, "Are we the ones to talk of trials and shrink from duty because the path is rough when we deserve nothing but hell?" She continued:

It is folly to think of ease and at the same time to be making way to that realm of eternal glory where conquerors are crowned with the reward of their victories.

I want more grace and feelings of entire consecration to God, to be willing to go where He marks the way, and take up the cross when He commands.

That she was a missionary at heart none can doubt. She wrote, "What Christian would not find it his constant happiness to be talking of the plan of salvation and meditating upon the character of Christ as exhibited on the cross!" She understood her primary role to be that of a helpmate: "That it is the duty of some females to be helpers in the great work of missions, I doubt not, and their influence there would doubtless be much greater than it could be at home." She drank deeply from the love of God manifest in Christ crucified:

But the simple fact that Jesus, the Lord of glory, has died to atone for the sins of men is sufficient to draw forth the admiration of every intelligent creature. What sinner of the

---

[33] Philippians 3:10

27

human race could not help but to forever dwell on this theme and be ever grateful to the condescending Savior?

I should sink down in final despair of heaven if I could not plead a hope for acceptance through the blood of Christ. Here is the Christian's only hope and O what a precious one! In Jesus there is an overflowing fullness, and eternity will not exhaust it.

When her health began to fail, her faith began to flourish. She wrote, "It certainly requires as much grace to suffer as it does to labor, and perhaps suffering is more necessary for us,[34] and better for the cause of Christ." She comforted another

---

[34] Editor's note: During suffering, it is helpful to meditate on the benefits of suffering. As one reflects on the benefits, comforts such as thanksgiving, praise, and new strength result. For example, suffering produces sanctification—as believers are humbled through suffering they learn to cling to Christ alone and walk in humility, becoming more like Him. Suffering produces mortification—it causes the believer to examine his heart to find specific sins that must be mortified so he can see the Lord (Heb. 12:14). Suffering produces compassion—those who are humbled by suffering no longer look with contempt on others who suffer but weep with those who weep (Rom. 12:15) and comfort others with the same comfort with which they are comforted by God (II Cor. 1:4). Suffering teaches hope—it removes the believer's hope from this life and realigns it to heaven. It teaches the believer to hope in Christ alone and the fullness of the reward He has purchased on the cross which will be given to him on that day (Romans 5:5; I Peter 1:3-7). Suffering teaches faith—it causes the believer to look beyond the temporal to the eternal—to believe that the Lord really intends this trial for the believer's good and will work it out for his pleasure with Christ in heaven. Suffering produces submission—it teaches the believer to humble himself under the mighty hand of God and submit to His good pleasure and will (I Peter 5:6). Suffering produces patience—it teaches the believer to submit to what God has allowed and to patiently wait on Him for relief or resolution (I Peter 5:6b; James 4:10). Suffering produces prayer—it causes the believer to become more acutely aware of his need for Christ and prompts him to call out to God for mercy day and night. Suffering produces humility—it causes the believer to see himself for who he really is—not strong or self-sufficient but a sinful, weak creature in need of the mercy of a great, holy, and mighty God.

28

missionary wife with the same comfort which she received from God:[35]

> Dear sister, how much we need the presence of Christ! Daily communion with Him would exclude proud aspiring thoughts and every murmuring wish. We should be happy and satisfied with anything He ordered, and those about us could not fail of being benefitted by our influence.

> The very first lesson to be learned is a patient, cheerful submission to circumstances; such circumstances as God, in infinite wisdom, permits to exist and in which He suffers His dear children to be placed.

She grieved over her limited involvement in the mission work. What she could not do for the people of Turkey in person, she did for them in prayer. She said, "We are in no danger of doing too much work in our closets, and perhaps we shall be as useful there as anywhere."

Elizabeth was an exemplary missionary. She did what few women in her generation were able to do—model on the mission field how to be a godly wife and mother. At her funeral, fellow missionary William Goodell said of her:

> She was a most faithful mother to her children. Notwithstanding her extreme debility, she daily attended to their instruction and seemed really to take delight in the performance of this duty. She prayed with them as well as for them. She taught them also to pray; and the eldest she had begun to teach to sing with her some of the songs of Zion. She seemed to feel that her family was a part of the great family of God, and that her children were to be trained up for

---

[35] II Corinthians 1:4

heaven rather than for earth—for eternity more than for time, and to have fellowship with the sons of God as well as with the sons of men.

Elizabeth fought the good fight,[36] refusing to surrender to fear. Communion with Christ was her portion and submission to His providence her strength. Trust in His goodness was her comfort and the consolations of the gospel her hope. Christ crucified was her theme and proclaiming His gospel her joy. Her children's conversion was her cry and raising them for missions her plea. Prayer was her "cord of maternal influence" and trust in God's promises her hope. Perseverance was her hallmark and employing the means of grace her privilege. Love for her children constrained her and confidence in God's promises cheered her. She was a completer to a contender for the faith in that she counted the cost of accompanying her husband to Turkey and concluded that Christ and His gospel are worth it. She suffered with a humble, submissive spirit and kept her eyes on the prize of the upward call of God in Christ Jesus.[37] As a missionary wife and mother, she bore on her body the brand-marks of the Lord Jesus,[38] which continued to preach the gospel to her children long after she was gone, forever testifying to Christ's beauty and displaying His worth.

ᘓ

---

[36] I Timothy 6:12
[37] Philippians 3:14
[38] Galatians 6:17

CHAPTER I

She Dwelt with Us in Love
A Summary of Elizabeth's Life

Mrs. Elizabeth B. Dwight was born to Joshua and Ruth Baker, of North Andover, Massachusetts in 1807. At an early age her mind was occupied with serious reflections, although there was little in her circumstances, so far as religious privileges were concerned, to direct her thoughts into such a channel. In her 16th year she became greatly distressed and was filled with terror in view of her sins and their prospective consequences. Her state of mind was peculiar. She was in constant fear and agitation, and could not bear to be left alone even for a moment, lest some terrible thing should happen to her. In the following year, her mind was quieted and occasionally cheered by the faint hope of pardoned sin. But the feeling was transient and soon gave way to deep despondency. During all this time she labored under great difficulties on account of the religious views of most around her who were of the Unitarian persuasion. She could not find a person who could direct her to the truth or who took the least interest in her spiritual condition. She was obliged to go alone, and some distance, to find a church where she could meet those with whom she could take sweet counsel and have free and satisfactory spiritual intercourse founded upon God's Word. This course was not only attended with much trouble, but it brought upon her great reproach from her family. Albeit, her mind at length became calm, and she sweetly trusted in the infinite merits of the Savior. It does not appear that her hopes were ever afterwards shaken, although she always maintained a godly suspicion over her own heart, ever awake to the danger of self deception in regard to her own religious character.

She united with the Congregational Church in South Andover, then under the pastoral care of the Rev. Justin Edwards, D. D., in the year 1826, as it is believed. In order to attend the ordinances, which to her were above all treasures, and to share in the fellowship of the believers, she was obliged to walk six miles from home and often endured severe reproach from her parents for doing so. This, however, was the school in which Providence trained her for the trials and hardships of the missionary life.

It appears that early on she purposed to devote herself to mission work if the Lord should open the way, although it is not known that she ever revealed her intention to any except her own beloved mother.

It may be proper to add, since that time, it is hoped that her father yielded up his heart to the Savior during his last sickness, his disease being consumption. Her mother still lives to bear testimony to the power of the gospel in supporting the soul under the sore trials of this present life. How much the instrumentality of the daughter was employed by the Holy Spirit in renovating the hearts of the parents will never be fully disclosed in this world, but it is believed that her example and godly conversation had great influence, and who can tell what blessings have come down in answer to her fervent prayers.

The following is an extract from a sermon preached by the Rev. William Goodell at Constantinople on the occasion of Elizabeth's death, to which will be added selections from some of her letters.

Elizabeth was married, January 1830, to the Rev. Harrison Dwight and sailed the same month for Malta, where she resided more than two years, and then relocated to Constantinople, where she spent the remainder of her short life. She has left a husband and three small children in this foreign land, the fourth child having gone immediately after her to the grave. In her native country, she left a widowed mother and two sisters, as well as a circle of correspondents and friends—all for whom we pray that the affliction may be greatly sanctified to them.

She always took pleasure in talking over the scenes of her early days, thus showing the deep and lively interest she still felt for home and country and the religious state of her friends and early companions.

Her mind was naturally strong, her conceptions clear, and her thoughts mature. Every effort she felt called upon to make was successful, as her letters to her native country bear ample testimony. A solid cultivation of mind by means of persevering and well directed study gave additional depth and interest to all she said. Everywhere a happy symmetry was perceptible in the training of her mind and heart, in natural gifts, acquired abilities, and gracious affections. She had a low opinion of herself. This was always manifested in everything she said and did. No person could be more unobtrusive than she was. No person could be farther than she from "sitting in the highest room."[39] She maintained a godly watch over her heart and was fearful of building on a sandy foundation[40] or of appearing to others to be what she was not in reality. So also, in conversing with others on their spiritual state, and especially with her children, she was careful not to encourage hopes which did not appear to her to be well founded. Some of the older children present can doubtless remember various anecdotes she at different times related of young persons about their own age who had been much affected by divine truth for a season but afterwards became as thoughtless as ever.

She was eminently patient. Her whole missionary life, from beginning to end, was one of great self-denial and suffering. But she submitted meekly to the affliction she was called upon to

---

[39] Luke 14:8
[40] Matthew 7:24-27

endure, and instead of indulging in a spirit of repining, she was enabled by divine grace to maintain a spirit of cheerfulness.

One of her last remarks in a note to a friend, after having alluded to her entire prostration of strength and to the difficulty of procuring help, was, "When we hear of a place where there are no trials or afflictions, we will both go together." Thus pleasantly did she turn off the subject of her own troubles. Her meaning was that this is a world of trial and affliction, and that no place or station is exempt from them. But, blessed be God! there is just such a place as she spoke of; and she was doubtless thinking of it at the very time with great comfort to herself, though it is not likely she was expecting to enjoy it so soon.

She was, emphatically, given to industry. This was the more remarkable, as she suffered so much from constant debility. She literally "did with her might whatever her hands found to do;"[41] and was thus able to accomplish more for her family than most mothers in like circumstances would be able to do. Not a fragment of time was suffered to be lost. And how often, by a little management, did she contrive to accomplish two things at once! From motives of economy, and with a view to save expense to the mission in every possible way, she often undertook to accomplish so much as to awaken the serious apprehensions of all her friends that she would injure her health. Her family cares were always many, and she was most careful to improve every moment, either with her needle, her book, her pen, or in trying to teach whoever might be disposed to learn; and all this without suffering things temporal to divert her attention from things eternal. It was her great desire to be useful. She left her country and pleasant home and came to this distant land with the hope of benefitting others; and her desire to be useful was ever leading her to go far beyond her strength. At different times she undertook the charge of a small school, but

---

[41] Ecclesiastes 9:10

her feeble health always obliged her to relinquish it. In one instance she attempted this when she already had the charge of two families besides her own; and all simply because she wished to do good. It was a great grief to her that she could do so little. It was in her heart to do much, but great bodily weakness prevented. Two years ago, after she had been brought very low by sickness, she said one day to an intimate Christian friend that she had felt as if her life was very unprofitable, and she was fast sinking into the grave; nor had she much desire to live, as she could accomplish so little good here, and as it would be such a happy thing to go to a world where she hoped to be forever free from sin and suffering; but just about that time there came from America a box containing books, cards, etc., for her children; "and now," she said, "I really wish to live a little longer, if it be the Lord's will, that I may have the privilege of instructing my own children, being now furnished with such additional helps." This leads to the remark that she was a most faithful mother to her children. Notwithstanding her extreme debility, she daily attended to their instruction and seemed really to take delight in the performance of this duty. She prayed with them as well as for them. She taught them also to pray; and the eldest she had begun to teach to sing with her some of the songs of Zion. She seemed to feel that her family was a part of the great family of God, and that her children were to be trained up for heaven rather than for earth—for eternity more than for time, and to have fellowship with the sons of God, as well as with the sons of men.

It was a source of peculiar pleasure to her that the Maternal Associations[42] in America felt so deep an interest in the children of missionaries; for she thought a missionary mother might now feel sure that her children, if left motherless in a strange land, would find faithful and affectionate friends among the mothers

---

[42] A group of mothers committed to meet together to pray for each other's children and to encourage one another in the high calling of motherhood

in the sweet home of her youth. And should our departed sister look into the "golden censer" in the hands of our great High Priest which is filled "with the prayers of all saints,"[43] may we not hope she will often have the pleasure of seeing prayers there from numerous Maternal Associations in America going up with a great cloud of incense in behalf of her own offspring?

In the Maternal Association that she began in Constantinople, she always manifested the most lively interest; and one of the last meetings she ever attended was a meeting of this society. This was only five days before her final illness. It devolved on her to conduct the exercises, and the hymn she selected to be sung on the occasion was the 23rd in the second book of Watts:

Descend from heaven, immortal Dove,
Stoop down and take us on Thy wings,
And mount, and bear us far above
The reach of these inferior things;

Beyond, beyond this lower sky,
Up where eternal ages roll,
Where solid pleasures never die,
And fruits immortal feast the soul.

O for a sight, a pleasant sight
Of our Almighty Father's throne!
There sits our Savior, crown'd with light,
Clothed in a body like our own.

Adoring saints around Him stand,
And thrones and powers before Him fall;
The God shines gracious through the man,
And sheds sweet glories on them all!

---

[43] Revelation 8:3

O what amazing joys they feel,
While to their golden harps they sing,
And sit on every heavenly hill,
And spread the triumphs of their King!

When shall the day, dear Lord, appear,
That I shall mount to dwell above;
And stand and bow among them there,
And view Thy face, and sing Thy love!

She remarked particularly on the line in the third verse: "There sits our Savior, crowned in light;" then referring to two other lines in another verse, she said, " 'Can it be that such sinners as we shall ere long sit on every heavenly hill and spread the triumphs of our King?' Can it be?" she said; and we respond, "It can be;"—it has been, in her own case. Who that knew her can doubt that it is even so? For if Christ has a kingdom in this world, we must believe she belonged to that kingdom. She acknowledged His authority; she lived in His empire, under His government; her name was entered on the catalogue of His subjects; all the laws and institutions of His holy kingdom were precious in her eyes; and all her tastes were in unison with those, not of the world, but of "the daughters of the Lord God Almighty."[44]

It was on the 27th of June that the plague entered the family and attacked Elizabeth and one of her children. The nature of the disease was not at first suspected. On the second day, the child, who lay in the same room with her, was supposed to be dying; but she was perfectly tranquil. Her own sufferings were great, but she uttered no complaint; she manifested a sweet resignation to the will of her heavenly Father as it respected the child. She afterwards, at different times, manifested by words or

---

[44] II Corinthians 6:18

37

signs, the same state of feeling with regard to herself; until one after another, speech, reason, strength, and finally, on the 12ᵗʰ day of her illness, life itself departed; and, being "absent from the body," we doubt not she is "present with the Lord."[45]

But what a change! Not from life to death, but from death to life! Why should we ever speak or think of her only as dead when she has gone to a world where there is absolutely no death and has in reality only now just begun to live? Her mind is no longer imprisoned in a feeble, diseased, dying body, and her moral powers are no longer oppressed and clogged by sin. She had her trials, her labors, and cares; but they are all ended. She had her distractions and interruptions, her days of languishing and nights of weariness, her doubts and fears, her watchings and fastings; but "the former things are passed away."[46] Time has brought an end to her sorrows, but eternity will bring no end to her joys. Our thoughts follow her to that "better country, even a heavenly one"[47] and, if we "love her, we shall rejoice because she has gone to the Father."[48] But our own loss we may and should mourn.

Next to her children, the loss to her husband is the greatest; and indeed he best, or rather he alone, knew all her worth. But his loss is her gain. And what is gain to her, especially such an infinite gain as this, may also be considered in one sense as gain to him; and if the providence be rightly improved, it will be gain to him in another and still more important sense. It was his privilege to accompany her to the banks of Jordan, attended by no other friend save the Friend of sinners; and that too with the almost certain prospect of being himself permitted to pass over to the promised land with her or immediately after.

But his hour was not yet come. The God who preserved Daniel in the lions' den and the three children in the furnace was

---

[45] II Corinthians 5:8
[46] II Corinthians 5:17
[47] Hebrews 11:16
[48] John 14:28

pleased to preserve him from the contagion of that dreadful disease to which he was so exposed and to restore him with the remnant of his family this day to our "solemn meeting." And shall we congratulate you, my brother, on what the world would call "a narrow escape from death"? No; we congratulate your children that they are not left without a father; we congratulate ourselves; and we render everlasting thanks to the great Head of the Church who hath heard and answered prayer. But it is not for ease and enjoyment, for rest and satisfaction, that you have been thus wonderfully preserved; but it is for further duties, cares, labors, trials, and dangers; perhaps even still greater ones than any you have yet had. And may we not hope that you also may be able to comfort others in their afflictions with the same comfort wherewith you yourself have been comforted of God in yours.[49]

To this mission, also, the loss is great. It is felt by every member of it, for to every member she was a sister much beloved. During the few short years she was connected with us, she dwelt with us in love; and who of us can point out a single instance when this love waxed cold?[50] Over "and above all" her other graces, she "put on charity, which is the bond of perfectness;"[51] and this sacred belt she not only "put on" but wore always. And what she is now in heaven we may consider, in one respect, as only the everlasting going on, carrying out, and perfecting of what she was here on earth. She lived with us here in love, and she has now gone to a world of love. In all her intercourse with us, whether the occasions were ordinary or extraordinary, she was always adorned with "the ornament of a meek and quiet spirit."[52]

---

[49] II Corinthians 1:4
[50] Matthew 24:12
[51] Colossians 3:14
[52] I Peter 3:4

Now, in the sight of God, this is not merely of value but of great value; and we doubt not, therefore, she will continue to wear it in His blessed presence forever. It is one of the loveliest graces of the Holy Spirit; a robe "clean and white;"[53] and as she never laid it aside in her intercourse with us here below, so we may be sure she will never lay it aside with the meek and lowly, the sanctified and sinless ones above.

The child, who was seized at the same time with the mother, survived the attack but forty-eight hours. And it is very remarkable that the last day of his life was the day on which it was his turn to be especially remembered, both here and at Broosa, in the precious little daily concert of prayer for the children of our families.[54] He continued in this world till we may suppose the last prayer was offered for him; and then, at half-past ten in the afternoon of the twenty-ninth of June, "he was not for God took him."[55]

Owing to a defect in his hearing, he was unable to speak, though he was more than two and a half years old and his mind was one of a high and most active order. His education, therefore, was becoming a subject of deep anxiety to his parents.

---

[53] Revelation 19:8

[54] This prayer meeting was commenced nearly two years ago in the family of Mr. Goodell, and the benefit of it being felt at once, it was extended immediately to embrace the children in all our families, both here and at Broosa. It takes a fortnight to go through with the whole list, and then the turn of the first on the list comes round again. On the two intervening Sabbaths, however, instead of making particular mention of our own children, we pray especially for the children of our friends at Smyrna, Trebizond, and Ooroomiah, and several Greek and Armenian families at Constantinople, being also at their own request included. This has been from the beginning a most interesting prayer concert to us all, and it has perhaps been quite as useful to the parents as the children. Three of those who were on the daily list, with two of those on the Sabbath list, have already ceased to be subjects of prayer. We feel, therefore, that we neither began to pray for the little ones too soon, nor that we have prayed for them too much, nor too fervently.

[55] Hebrews 11:5

But he now has a teacher who can gain full access to his fine understanding, and under whose instruction he has doubtless learned more already than he would ever have learned in this world, even though his advantages should have been the best possible, and though his life should have been prolonged to the term of as many centuries as was common in the antediluvian age.

∞

CHAPTER II

Preparing to Die

Elizabeth's Missionary Call and Passion

The views with which Elizabeth entered the mission field may be gathered from the following letters, written while she was still in America. A very prominent trait in her character which all observed who knew her was a low opinion of herself. With a clear, strong, and well cultivated mind, she united a heart truly devoted to God; and yet it was her nature to shrink from observation and to feel that others would do far better than herself in any given sphere of labor. She never seemed sensible of the strength of her own powers or of the success of her own efforts. Soon after the question of a personal engagement in missions was proposed to her, she wrote to a friend as follows, under date of Andover, March 12, 1828:

The more the missionary enterprise is reflected upon, the more it seems of vast, incomprehensible magnitude, and I shrink from a personal engagement in the work, with a sense of utter inability and unworthiness. Nevertheless it is a work that has engaged the most earnest desires of my heart, and if I am not deceived, to which I would most willingly devote my strength and whatever God may have bestowed upon me; and I would hope that even life might not seem too dear a sacrifice. But the feebleness of my Christian hope and the weakness of my faith often lead to many distressing fears, lest if the lot should be mine to go to some heathen clime, I should faint and sink in the hour of trial, and thus wound the cause of the dear Redeemer. But blessed be His name for the assurance that in Him we may have righteousness and strength, and that as our day is, so shall our strength be.[56] I desire to feel and rejoice in an entire dependence on God. I have endeavored to bring to the test the motives of my heart that would lead me to the heathen. I have great reason for doubt, but cannot be prevailed upon to think that worldly inducements would be the cause of my decision to leave the friends of my youthful days, so ardently loved, to enter on a scene of unknown trials and sorrows. With my present feelings, I cannot refuse my feeble aid to the cause of Christ and still be happy.

The following extract is from a letter on the same subject, dated Andover, March 26, 1828:

To a mind of tender sensibility, the idea is almost insupportable of bidding farewell to friends, dear as life itself, and leaving forever the scenes of early days around which there is thrown a magic charm; but when we are led to feel that it is what God commands, and when the appalling condition of the poor perishing arises to view, and the worth of only one soul is contemplated, the thought of trials vanishes, and no sacrifice seems too great if we can but meliorate their state.

Having been retired and alone this day, my thoughts have been more exclusively devoted to examining the correctness of former conclusions. That it is the duty of some females to be helpers in the great work of missions, I doubt not, and their influence there would doubtless be much greater than it could be at home. There are also a sufficient number who are willing to remain in their own happy country.

_____

[56] Deuteronomy 33:25

I can see at present no obstacles in the way of going but a sad insufficiency. No claim appears greater than that which 600,000,000 of perishing people present. It is the want of a heart expanded with holy benevolence, intent upon the glory of God, and absorbed in the interests of the Redeemer's kingdom, that makes me hesitate and tremble, though God I know will not desert His own dear children in the hour of need.

After she had fully determined that duty bid her to enter the missionary field, she wrote as follows from Salem, May 23, 1828:

Though I am always in doubt of my Christian hope and am often unhappy for want of that holy confidence which results from being near to God, yet, all things considered, I have not once regretted my determination. If God has anything in the climes of unreached peoples for so unworthy an instrument to accomplish, may He prepare me for the work and send me forth; and if not, make me submissive to His will.

I have often many hours of anxiety, fearing that when distressing afflictions come, "I shall sink into the deep waters."[57] But if we cannot endure the trials and sorrows of life, what shall we do when we come in the deep swellings of Jordan?[58] That cold stream all must ford. There is no possibility of avoiding it wherever we may dwell. There will be grief enough in any state to sink the heart without divine assistance. And where are we most likely to meet with this? Is it not when in the path of duty? This then would be our safest and best way, even if our motive were mere personal happiness. It is folly to think of ease and at the same time to be making way to that realm of eternal glory where

---

[57] Psalm 69:2
[58] A reference to death

conquerors are crowned with the reward of their victories. "Through much tribulation we must enter into the kingdom of heaven."[59] Blessed is the assurance that though "many are the afflictions of the righteous, but the Lord will deliver him out of all."[60]

The following extracts from about the same time as above disclose her views on some important subjects:

It is good to feel an implicit reliance on the will of God. We do best to walk by faith.[61] This grace the missionary peculiarly needs, for without it he will sink when he comes into the deep waters of affliction.[62] We should, indeed, wherever our lot may be in the world, keep the command in view, "Be ye holy, for I am holy;"[63] for we shall need for our own souls, at the hour of death, if never before, all the faith and holiness we can attain. But a world lying in wickedness[64] calls for our unremitted exertions in its behalf; and if we would do good we must "grow in grace,"[65] die daily[66] to sin and "live unto righteousness."[67] O that we may feel like Paul when he exclaimed, "I desire to depart and be with Christ,"[68] and yet be willing to abide in the flesh for the sake of the churches. Then the world will feel our influence, and ages yet to come may "bless God that we once lived."

I wish I felt more pity for the wretched condition of perishing souls and more earnest desires to be made the

---

[59] Acts 14:22
[60] Psalm 34:19
[61] II Corinthians 5:7
[62] Psalm 69:14
[63] I Peter 1:16
[64] I John 5:19
[65] II Peter 3:18
[66] I Corinthians 15:31
[67] I Peter 2:24
[68] Philippians 1:23

favored instrument of salvation to them. It is not right to indulge our selfish feelings and enjoy contentedly, alone, the blessings which are granted to us while thousands are perishing in want of them. Heaven will at length call for the improvement we make of every one of its gifts and be impartial in its retribution.

I do not in secret mourn that the way of my future life in prospect seems full of labors, trials, and crosses, nor wish to be permitted to pass my days in ease and in the fullness of earthly comforts. No; I want more grace and feelings of entire consecration to God, to be willing to go where He marks the way, and take up the cross when He commands. If He has anything for me to do in a foreign country, I hope I am willing to go forth as soon as may be necessary.

I do believe the time will come when holiness to the Lord[69] will be written on all the Christian possesses. I have long been wishing that this might be the case with whatever gift heaven may have granted me, however humble a one it may be in comparison of those with which it may have favored others.

I have lived at a poor dying rate and have not in anything done my duty; if I am like anyone, I am like Peter, following Jesus from afar. Though this is the sad truth concerning myself, I love better the friend who lives and acts uniformly and decidedly for God.

In another one of her letters she wrote:

O what excellence appears in the religion of Christ when we view it supporting the soul in the dark hour of dissolution— when every earthly prop sinks and friends stand aloof, when those who have had many doubts and fears find them all

---

[69] Exodus 28:36

gone, and are enabled to say, "death, where is thy sting! grave, where is thy victory!"[70] — O, will the consolations of the gospel be ours in that hour? Will the Friend of sinners light up the dark valley as we walk through it? No matter then if far away from the home of our relatives we sicken, languish, and die—no matter if friends around are few and o'er our dying couch alone should watch the tawny strangers of another land.

That the love of Christ constrained her appears from the following selections written in April and June of the year 1828:

There is something delightful in the thought of telling to the poor heathen the story of redeeming love. The mystery cannot be explained. This remains to be unfolded in eternity. But the simple fact that Jesus, the Lord of glory, has died to atone for the sins of men, is sufficient to draw forth the admiration of every intelligent creature. What sinner of the human race could not help but to forever dwell on this theme and be ever grateful to the condescending Savior! O that it were thus that all did feel and acknowledge this debt of gratitude! What Christian would not find it his constant happiness to be talking of the plan of salvation and meditating upon the character of Christ as exhibited on the cross!

I should sink down in final despair of heaven if I could not plead a hope for acceptance through the blood of Christ. Here is the Christian's only hope and O what a precious one! Defiled and polluted as we are, and imperfect as are all our actions here, a way is opened to restore us to the image of God, to purify us in His sight, and to fit us for His holy presence. In Jesus there is an overflowing fullness, and

---

[70] I Corinthians 15:55

eternity will not exhaust it. O, if we have received of this fullness, how grateful should we be! How earnest to redeem our time[71] and cause the world to feel our holy influence; to show to all around our sorrow for the evil we have done, and that as we have been the servants of sin,[72] so now we wish to be of holiness![73]

Shall we not count it all joy to suffer for Jesus[74]—to consecrate every talent to His service and make every possible exertion for the promotion of His cause? He demands this, and He has a right to it. Are we the ones to talk of trials and shrink from duty because the path is rough, when we deserve nothing but hell? O if we could feel the worth of souls and our obligations to God, as we shall when the light of eternity bursts upon our minds, how widely different would be all that we think, say, and do! The world would then say of us that we had indeed been with Jesus.[75] Then we should wish for ten thousand times the faculties we now possess, that in the flow of our gratitude to the Savior and pity for perishing sinners, we might employ them all in labors of benevolence. May the Spirit of God enlighten and warm our hearts so that we shall spend our few remaining days in the manner we shall wish they had been spent when we stand at the bar of God!"

A friend had related to her a very affecting case of a young merchant who had the reputation of eminent holiness, but who soon after an unfavorable turn in his commercial affairs, forsook the people of God, became intemperate, espoused openly the cause of infidelity, and devoted himself to public efforts for the overthrow of that faith which he once professed. Elizabeth

---

[71] Ephesians 5:16
[72] Romans 6:20
[73] Romans 6:19
[74] James 1:2
[75] Acts 4:13

wrote the following in answer to a request for her opinion on the case, under date of Salem, June 14, 1828:

> My soul shuddered on reading the relation you gave of the condition of a certain individual; for the first thought was that he might be one of those unhappy creatures for whom "there remains no more sacrifice for sins, but a certain fearful looking for of judgment and fiery indignation."[76] This I would not say, however; and by no means would I limit the mercy of God in his case. I know not what conclusion to draw. The sequel of his life, no doubt, will furnish means for a much more satisfactory determination than can now be made. "It is impossible," saith the apostle, "for those who were once enlightened, and have tasted of the heavenly gift, etc., if they shall fall away, to renew them unto repentance."[77]
>
> I do not suppose this to refer to real Christians. That they do sometimes fall into gross and open iniquity, the examples of Scripture testify; and I suppose they may remain for some time at ease, taking no thought of their guilt; and that they may continue for a considerable length of time in the practice of some darling sin. The question is, how far can one proceed in sin and still be a Christian? This limit I cannot assign. I confess I can hardly conceive it possible that one who has been born of the Spirit should live for some years in the habitual indulgence of the most debasing crimes and at the same time attempt to build up a religion in opposition to that which the Spirit has taught him. And now you must tell me your opinion of the case in question. If the world has so strong a possession of the heart that an interruption of its sunshine will cause one in his madness to abandon himself to vice, which does that soul love most—Christ or the world?

---

[76] Hebrews 10:27
[77] Hebrews 6:4, 6

And "if any man love the world, the love of the Father is not in him."[78] Would anyone have supposed, after having seen Judas act in the character of an apostle and apparently possessing the spirit of a true disciple, that he could have betrayed his Master? Was it not because of the distinguishing grace of God that the others fell not but were supported through fiery trials and enabled to remain firm and unyielding, even unto death? And if you or I ever reach the heavenly Jerusalem, our song must be "Grace, free grace!" "Not unto us, Lord, but to Thy name be all the glory!"[79] It becomes us, then, to rejoice with trembling,[80] and take heed lest God should be provoked to withdraw from us His sustaining grace.

ॐ

---

[78] I John 2:15
[79] Psalm 115:1
[80] Psalm 2:11

CHAPTER III

On the Field

Harrison and Elizabeth Arrive in Turkey

Constantinople, June 22, 1832

My dear Mother and Sisters,

I doubt not but you will be glad to hear that we are at Constantinople, though we are now farther removed from you, as you may perhaps have indulged some anxiety in regard to our passage. . . . We cannot but feel under peculiar obligations of gratitude to God for His goodness in preserving us, both from falling prey to the hands of pirates and from the danger of the deep. The constant rocking of the vessel, and almost everything about a ship, I dislike. It is well that many people think otherwise; and it would be better if I and all others, like the Apostle Paul, could learn, "in whatsoever situation we are therewith to be content."[81]

We are still residing with Mr. Goodell's family, but shall live by ourselves as soon as we can obtain a house. House rent is exceedingly expensive, and the customs of society are totally the reverse of good American ways. Every family of respectability must have a train of servants. How we shall get along, I do not know. I cannot easily think of having a servant to constantly supervise, and I am concerned about the negative influence a servant might have upon our little James Harrison, for he is now a good boy.

If the Lord wills, we expect to work among the Armenians. I must begin immediately to study the Armenian language, which is doubtless hard. We hope the way will soon be opened for the commencement of schools among the Armenians.

---

[81] Philippians 4:11

I cannot tell you my feelings when I first entered Turkey and beheld a Turkish village. It seemed like an assemblage of huts. But I hope to tell you more hereafter, and that I am more profitably employed than heretofore for the good of perishing sinners. If I can be useful here, I shall be happy. When I look around upon such a multitude of deluded souls, I feel myself to be indeed in a wilderness of sin and misery. Do pray for us continually, and O my dear sisters, do improve your privileges.

Here is James Harrison's pencil mark. I have also put in a lock of his hair—it is becoming darker now. I have got this paper already crowded, and have not said half I wish. Do not let any one see this—it has been written in very great haste. Love to all dear friends. I hope to hear that many I love have become pious during the wonderful effusion of the Holy Spirit in New England. Love to Mrs. Harris, and the dear Hastleton family; to cousin Holt and wife; and to Dr. Johnson and wife. My dear husband sends love to you all.

Yours very affectionately,
Elizabeth B. Dwight

Constantinople, Aug. 30, 1832
My dear Miss K.,

In this city there is one who often thinks of you, though you may not be aware of it. Where are you, dear Miss K.? What are you doing? I hope you are not living in idleness like the people of this country. This disposition, I am happy to know, is not a general trait of the American character, and it ought never to manifest itself in the Christian. Perhaps you are dwelling in sweet tranquility at your father's house and are fulfilling there the duties of piety; or shall I imagine that you have chosen another home even more dear—that of a husband! I long to hear from you!

We hear wonderful and rejoicing news concerning the prosperity of Zion in the United States; some of which you have probably witnessed. Has not your cup of delight been overflowing? Perhaps some individuals from your nearest connections for whose salvation you have long prayed, often with weeping, have been brought to the feet of Christ and have tasted that the Lord is indeed gracious.[82]

We arrived in this city last June, after a passage of three weeks from Malta. Our residence at that island was very pleasant, though the long period of my husband's absence was quite trying. The separation from our missionary friends and other acquaintances we had formed in that place was painful. Among other friends was a young lady, the daughter of an English magistrate, a most lovely and intelligent girl of ardent piety and unaffected simplicity, from whom we parted with much regret.

We are now living in a village on the Bosphorus inhabited chiefly by Armenians, though we daily see different sorts of people and hear a variety of languages spoken. In Malta, my health was very miserable much of the time, and with the care of my babe, I was not able to study—I only picked up a little Italian, and of course I am now sometimes rather troubled when meeting with people of an unknown tongue.

We intend to direct our efforts to the Armenians and hope by and by to have schools established among them. Light and knowledge advance very slowly as yet in these countries. My dear husband is employed in studying the Armenian language, which perhaps I may attempt after a while. I am now taking French lessons. Mr. Goodell's family lives in the same house with us, and Mrs. Goodell is the only female companion who speaks English. She is a very sweet and amiable woman.

Our dear little boy, James Harrison, is nearly two years old, and runs in the garden all the day for amusement. He is just beginning to learn his letters. I suppose you will hardly be able to believe this! Forgive me, my dear friend, for having intruded so

---

[82] I Peter 2:3

long upon your patience, and I beg you will reply very soon. Please remember me to your sisters. Harrison joins me in love to you.

Yours, very affectionately,
Elizabeth B. Dwight

Constantinople, Sept. 6, 1832

My dear Mother and Sisters,

We are now living in a village called Pela Raje among the Armenians, in the same house with Mr. and Mrs. Goodell. Mr. Schauffler and Mr. Paspati board here as well. We set the dinner table every night for fifteen persons.

We are obliged to keep pretty much shut up from the natives as the plague is now raging, and there is no danger of getting this disease but by contact. The infection often remains in clothes a long time and perhaps is more frequently passed by them more than anything else. When the gentlemen have been out they smoke their clothes immediately on coming into the house, as this is said to be a certain destroyer of the infection, and we dare buy nothing except what can bear to be scalded in water or washed in vinegar. We have been glad to hear of no case in this village for eleven days. Many families in which the plague has been are living now in tents about a quarter of a mile from the house.

You will perhaps think it strange if I tell you I indulge but little apprehension about this disease, but so it is, that when living in the midst of evils we lose our fears. But our only hope is in the protection of God. Our house stands at the head of the street and is surrounded by a high wall. There is a pleasant garden connected with it which contains a variety of fruit, though not a great abundance, such as pears, peaches, plums, figs, pomegranates, cherries, grapes, and quinces. Quinces grow in great abundance and are very large and fair. Adjoining the

56

garden is a long vineyard filled with grapes and the finest fruit, in which we can walk at any time, and the owner sends us often a large platter of fruit. I dare to eat but little of it yet, though I enjoy tolerably good health. Little James Harrison enjoys it very much. He has his hat on and runs in the garden from morning till night.

Yesterday we took a Greek girl to help in the home. I can only talk with her by signs. . . . Sewing is something we have to do frequently in this place, and I have not had a little amount to do for my family, though I have had no assistance.

"'Vanity of vanities,' saith the preacher, 'all is vanity.'"[83] There is folly and sin enough in any country, but in some places there is light, and there are people who walk with God in the rich ordinances of the gospel by which the soul is nourished. My dear mother and sisters, while you have the light, walk in it,[84] and let us bless God forever for His distinguishing goodness. My time is very much occupied—I am studying French, and I must begin immediately, if my health is continued. I also need to study Greek and Armenian. I do not expect to know or speak all of these languages at present, but a missionary needs them all or an equal number here. I meet persons almost daily to whom I cannot speak a word, and thus make a very awkward appearance, besides other disadvantages.

My husband sends much love to you all, as well as myself.

Yours very affectionately,
Elizabeth

---

83 Ecclesiastes 1:2
84 John 12:35

Constantinople, Feb. 3, 1834

My dear Miss P.,

Your letter was received some time last April and read with those emotions of pleasure which you will know better how to conceive when finding yourself indeed an "isolated being" in some foreign land.

O that some little winged messenger could drop in this evening with dispatches dictated this very morning from you. What tidings might he bring! Such as would cheer us all in our solitude and inspire the delightful delusion of tasting the sweets of Christian conversation and love at the fireside of a dear friend in America? Or would he tell a tale of sorrow in which our hearts would painfully sympathize? I can hardly think of friends across the Atlantic under any other circumstances than those of comfort and prosperity, so liberally does heaven scatter its blessings upon our happy country. But experience assures me that sorrow in its turn more or less frequently finds it way to every breast. The Christian however has an antidote ever at hand, "a balm for every wound."[85]

We rejoice to believe that the Spirit of God is causing many wonderful and blessed changes among our people at home. And as the work of God goes on there, we have reason to believe it will be promoted in other lands and among nations yet ignorant of the gospel. The mercy of Christ, in answer to fervent prayer, will open a hundred doors of usefulness in every direction and provide laborers to sow the seed or reap the harvest. I trust, dear friend, we have your special prayers for us and this mission, and be assured we value them more than silver or gold. We need above everything else the Spirit of God to dwell in our own hearts and to be poured out upon those around us. Then we might expect to see the Muslim, the Jew, the Greek, the Turk,

---

[85] Jeremiah 8:22

and all who are perishing becoming followers of the meek and lowly Jesus.

We are not without some evidence that the efforts made here, feeble as they are, meet the acceptance of our heavenly Father; but O, if we had more faith, how would a gracious shower descend instead of a few drops!

We are now greatly encouraged and strengthened by the arrival of a few warm-hearted brethren and sisters—Mr. and Mrs. Schneider, Mr. and Mrs. Johnson, Mr. and Mrs. Perkins, and Mrs. Schauffler. I think you would be pleased to see what a pleasant little circle of Americans there is in this great and far distant city of Constantinople. Last Wednesday evening we all met at the house of Commodore Porter upon a special occasion; no less than that of the wedding of Mr. Schauffler and Miss Reynolds of the Smyrna mission. It was a scene of solemn and lively interest, and the opportunity was improved in a profitable manner.

Our residence is now in Pera among the Frank population, which is a mixture of all nations, and the predominant faith among them is the Roman Catholic; and of course, but few of them have any friendship for Protestant missionaries. The females are devoted to fashion and dissipation, and I am told are extremely limited in their ideas. I teach the Scriptures to a small group of sweet children whose mothers are Roman Catholics and whose fathers are English Protestants. They speak but little English except what they have learned at school, but I hope they have already treasured up some portions of Scripture and hymns which they may not soon forget. Harrison and I also have some Armenian pupils—he has the gentlemen, and I have the boys and one girl, whom we are educating. Of the former, we hope two have been taught of the Spirit of God, and that he is preparing them for His own service.

I wish you could step into our room just now and see how literary we look. No less than three are studying the Turkish grammar, and a fourth is teaching Armenian to a servant. I begin to find out I am a dunce as to learning to talk new languages. A change of circumstances obliges me to change speaking from Italian to Greek, and from this to Turkish, and then to French, whilst amid family duties, etc. I can find scarcely a moment to study any language. I am sure you would be delighted with the Turkish, it is so noble and harmonious, and though it is hard to read, your perseverance would soon overcome it. In the Arabic character, which is the proper one, the vowels are suppressed; and in the Armenian character there is no dictionary. French is the popular language of the people in Pera.

You would be delighted to know that the Lord has blessed us with two dear little ones! Our youngest, William Buck, is ten months old, and our oldest, James Harrison, is two and a half. When you think of us, please pray for them, that they may be saved from their sins and the polluting examples of this country.

How is your Hebrew coming along? I despair of ever undertaking such a work, however delightful it would be. I thank you for the papers. Please inform Miss S. and Miss K. of the reception of a letter from them which I hope some time to find a moment to answer. My love continues the same to you all, though I cannot write as often as I wish. Do write as often as possible, and believe me ever,

Your affectionate friend,
Elizabeth B. Dwight

P.S. Harrison unites in the best regards to yourself, your parents, and other friends.

CHAPTER IV

Missions in and through the Home

Elizabeth's Devotion to Her Children

Elizabeth entered the missionary field with high expectations of the direct influence she should have upon the souls of the distressed and perishing. However, early in her missionary career her health failed, and she ever afterwards remained an invalid.

Her disease was a chronic diarrhea, accompanied by some other debilitating complaints. The consequence was a bitter disappointment in regard to the active labor she had marked out for herself, to which she submitted only after repeated efforts made at the expense of her strength and health to accomplish the object of her desires. This will be gathered from some of the letters which follow.

Notwithstanding the discouraging nature of her complaints, she maintained a degree of energy and courage that were quite remarkable. Her physician, who knew well the character of her disease, expressed great surprise at her activity a short time previous to her last illness.

The following was written to a beloved missionary sister who was suffering from similar weaknesses, with whom she deeply sympathized. The letter from which the extract is taken was dated Constantinople, Feb. 19, but of what year it does not appear:

Alas! how many disappointments succeed our long cherished hopes and plans! But if we would only learn by them to lean more implicitly on our Divine Shepherd, leaving tomorrow to take care of itself,[86] it would be no matter. You and I have

---

[86] Matthew 6:34

both seen the futility of our plans in the missionary life to a certain extent, and I hope we shall be submissive and cheerful, let what will come, and glorify God in whatever way He chooses.

Again, in another letter to the same person, dated August 8, 1836, she says in reference to some evil forebodings in regard to her own debilitated state:

I am afraid it is a want of submission to the will of God that suffers such thoughts to prevail, and I try to get rid of them; but sins and sorrows cleave fast to one, especially the former.

It certainly requires as much grace to suffer as it does to labor, and perhaps suffering is more necessary for us, and better for the cause of Christ.

I cannot do even the one half that is needful for the instruction of our own dear children; and then to think how much might be done for perishing souls around us, and to be able to accomplish nothing, is truly humbling. How different this is from the picture of a missionary life as we viewed it in America!

Dear sister, how much we need the presence of Christ! Daily communion with Him would exclude proud aspiring thoughts and every murmuring wish. We should be happy and satisfied with anything He ordered, and those about us could not fail of being benefitted by our influence.

Once more, in reference to the breaking up of a small school that she had just commenced, but which her state of health did not allow her to continue, she wrote to another missionary sister, Mrs. Susan Schneider, under date of Constantinople, Dec. 14, 1835:

I sometimes feel sad in not being able to go on with what I had began, but it is all perfectly right. Moderation—moderation is the lesson I am obliged to learn from morning until night, and from day to day.

A little more exertion than usual, one step in indulgence in eating, or a new source of anxiety, is sufficient to make me sick. I feel exceedingly concerned for our dear sister P. I wrote her a long letter last week, but I am afraid it will not produce the impression I intended. I wished to caution her from my own experience to be exceedingly careful in everything that could affect her health. I have no doubt she is careful, above many others, yet after all, her desire to be active and useful may sometimes lead her to overstep the bounds of prudence. Do try, sister, to keep her back, and do not undertake too much yourself. There is a strong temptation in such a land of darkness and ignorance to overdo ourselves in labor.

We are in no danger of doing too much work in our closets, and perhaps we shall be as useful there as anywhere. How many souls might we carry to Jesus if we possessed the faith and zeal of Paul, of David Brainerd, or of many Christians in the ordinary walks of life! O that the Spirit would come among us by His almighty, converting influences! What can we desire more than this blessing? What is all the universe to us weak missionaries without it? I do hope we all feel our need more than we have done. I know and confess that I have not encouraged and held up the hands of my brethren and sisters as I ought,[87] and I feel condemned before God.

To a missionary sister who recently entered into the field, she wrote as follows:

---

[87] Exodus 17:12

There is no driving forward through all hazards on missionary ground as one is apt to imagine beforehand. The very first lesson to be learned is a patient, cheerful submission to circumstances; such circumstances as God, in infinite wisdom, permits to exist, and in which He suffers His dear children to be placed. How many of our brethren and sisters in the missionary field have almost on their first outset lost a large portion of their health and energy to labor! How few of them have not! And how many sainted spirits are now around the throne of God who just a short time ago were actively engaged in the same enterprise in which we are now enlisted! If all these admonitions cannot stir us up to be faithful in self-preparation for eternity and move us to prayer and labor as far as our strength will allow for the salvation of those around us, what can?

Now a question of some importance is suggested by the preceding extracts—namely, to what extent ought the wife of a missionary engage in direct and active efforts for the good of the people around her? Although this is not the place to enter at large into an examination of this subject, yet a few considerations may with propriety be suggested. It is certain that no higher standard of action should be set up than the truth will bear. There is no gain, but a real and distressing loss, in acting contrary to this rule. The plea that human nature is so sluggish that it becomes necessary to present a very high point of aim in order to raise it to anything like its proper degree of action has no application here. It is never necessary, and never proper, to point men to a standard of action above their duty. Our Savior never did this.

He never told men that they must love Him with two hearts in order to secure from them the affections of one. He always directed them exactly to the point to which they were in duty bound to come; and more than this He never required on any

64

pretence, nor was He ever satisfied with less. We should always bear this in mind and remember that we may do as much injury by exaggerating as by diminishing the claims of duty. In the case before us we have no express directions in the Word of God; of course we are to decide the question on general principles and by a reference to circumstances.

That the wife of a missionary should go forth with higher views than of simply being the purveyor of her husband's table and the superintendent of his wardrobe is plain. The station is one of deep importance and of high responsibility. She is set up as a spectacle for the world to scrutinize; she should therefore be of such a character as will bear inspection. She is also to be the companion and counselor of her husband, perhaps the only one he has; for this, qualifications of a high order are necessary. She should also, by her education and mental endowments, be prepared to exert an influence on the people around her in whatever way the providence of God may direct.

We believe, however, that in the great majority of cases, it must be expected that her principal direct efforts will be made in her own household. She may have some sort of a general supervision over schools, but it must not be supposed to be her duty to engage for any length of time personally in the instruction of schools. This some married ladies have done, and a few may do it regularly and permanently; but these are rare exceptions and are not to be regarded as forming a rule. The subject of schools is mentioned because this is one of the most common and obvious means supposed to belong to the sphere of a female missionary.

In order to render the case more palpable, let us put the question to our Christian sisters at home who have families, and ask them, what are the difficulties of devoting three to six hours a day to teaching school and managing the home? And when they have enumerated them all, then we are ready to assent, and to prove too, that on missionary ground these difficulties are incalculably greater.

1. A foreign climate, in most cases, seriously affects the health if special care is not taken; and the missionary's wife, especially, needs to proceed with great moderation. She cannot put forth half the strength that she could in America with impunity.

2. There are difficulties in the way of the proper management of her household affairs owing to the customs of the people, which can never be appreciated at home, but which form a serious obstacle to much out-door labor.

3. The education of her children depends, as a general thing, almost wholly upon herself. If she does not devote herself to their instruction, they will never be instructed. And what is of still more consequence, if her watchful care and sedulous attentions are withdrawn only for a short time, they readily relapse into bad habits, influenced by the bad examples around them, and are in danger of falling an easy prey to temptations unknown in America. Here is a subject broad, deep, and vast, which calls forth the anxieties, occupies the thoughts, and excites the prayers of the missionary mother to a degree that is known only to God who searches the hearts. Whatever is left undone for the people around her, she cannot abandon her own offspring to ignorance, folly, and sin. It should also be remarked that she cannot, as might be supposed by some, instruct them together with native children in the same school. In almost every case, so close an alliance with native children would prove injurious; and furthermore, the language of her instructions to her own children must be the English, which would not of course be that of a native school.

As to the direct efforts for the salvation of the people around her, besides school-teaching, the missionary's wife must of course be guided by circumstances. If her health is ordinarily good, and Providence opens the door, she may do much by occasional visits among the people and by receiving them into her own home. Various other modes of usefulness will suggest themselves, as they do to Christian females in America. In most cases, however, for the reasons above stated, these efforts must be irregular and often interrupted, and she must for the most part be content to be a keeper at home.[88] Will it be said that it is good therefore for a missionary not to marry? It is answered that, for various reasons, he needs a wife far more than if he were to remain at home. Experience has fully settled this point, and it is so generally acknowledged that it is not necessary to devote any time to it in this place.

Few missionaries are more tenderly alive to the wants of those around them than was Elizabeth. In schools and other direct labors for them, it may emphatically be said of her—she hath done what she could.[89] Nay, she often went beyond her strength in these labors, until a painful experience checked her benevolent course and taught her those useful lessons of moderation which she afterwards endeavored to inculcate upon others.

She was a most tender, watchful, vigilant mother, and the feeling of responsibility in regard to her children evidently deepened as she contemplated the subject and her little ones advanced in years. She had four children—all boys—the eldest being seven years and the youngest only four months old at the time of her departure.

One of these however, two and a half years of age, had followed her in flight the following day.

ॐ

---

[88] Titus 2:5
[89] Mark 14:8

CHAPTER V

Educating Children for the Church

Elizabeth's Vision for Her Children

The following letters show something of Elizabeth's views of parental responsibility.

Constantinople, Sept. 4, 1835

My dear Madam,

I embrace the earliest opportunity of replying to your very kind favor of March 19, 1835. Had it been an ordinary letter of friendship coming from your hand, it would have been highly prized and have entitled you to my sincere thanks. But touching, as it does, the chord of maternal love, it calls forth my whole soul, and tears rise unbidden while I attempt to address you.

As the subject of training up our children for the Lord is the theme on which you have mainly dwelt, and the one in which we are united by a common bond, I shall immediately enter upon it and introduce ourselves to your notice without further apology.

I trust we are all thankful for such a privilege of presenting our case before a group of praying mothers in Israel and beseeching them to bear us and our offspring with their own before the mercy-seat.

We met last week—Mrs. Goodell, Mrs. Schauffler, and myself—though only three in number, we formed ourselves into a "Maternal Association," adopting your constitution, as far as our circumstances would admit. . . . Mrs. Schneider and Mrs. Powers at Broosa requested to be made members of an association with us, and we accordingly consider them as such, though indeed they are a hundred miles away! They engage to observe the same time as we to meet for prayer, and to remember often in their supplications each child by name, as well as to assist in maintaining a regular correspondence. Mrs.

Schneider has a little girl born last April, but Mrs. Powers is not a mother, except at heart.

You will, perhaps, wonder that our minds have so long lain dormant upon this important subject; and on reviewing the past, we wonder at ourselves for so much inactivity. The smallness of our number has presented itself as a discouragement, though we did once last winter meet expressly for the purpose of forming a society and were interrupted. Since then we have had numerous hindrances; one of us being either sick or situated at a distance from the rest.

And now, dear madam, if the weight of maternal responsibility almost crushes mothers in America, blessed with every facility for enlightening the minds of their children and purifying their own hearts, and surrounded with all the means of grace, what think you a Christian mother in this land of spiritual darkness must feel? How often must her closet testify to "groanings that cannot be uttered,"[90] in behalf of her children; and her pillow be moistened with tears of grief when the world is hushed!

Would that, with one effort, I could hold up to your view the moral picture of the society in which we live! Alas! would one well-regulated Christian family be seen to stand out in bold relief upon the dark picture? I almost fear not. Where would you behold a temple to Jehovah unpolluted with the grossest idolatry? Where a Bible class, church meeting, or maternal prayer association? Where would you find even a school of virtue and knowledge that has not been fostered by the charities and nurtured by the prayers of Christians in foreign lands?

Add to this destitution of the means of education all the pomp of a false religion, massive church buildings, glittering with gold and silver, blazing with lights, filled with crowds of devotees, bowing to the images of saints, a numerous priesthood

---

[90] Romans 8:26

clothed with the ensigns of power and pride, stamped with the name of holy, and you will have a faint idea of the reality.

A mother must be the model and almost the only model of virtue and religion her children will have. She must be their teacher, their companion, their playmate, their nurse, and every thing else. Her little ones must live in her presence from morning till night, whether she is sick or well. If she goes to the throne of grace, her children must be by her side, or her heart will be drawn away by the thoughts of their physical or moral danger. If she goes to church meetings,[91] her children must go too; if she visits the sick or the lost, they must be of the party, or the servants will teach them to dance, lie, or deceive, if they are left at home.

Children are much more minute observers than their parents are generally aware of. The first detection of what is going wrong in the house is usually from a simple-hearted remark or query from them, or the evil is embodied forth in their actions. No sooner has the pompous procession of priests displaying the holy cross followed by a train of boys bearing torches and singing through the nose their monstrous notes passed our windows, than our children are marching about the room with their sticks raised, chanting the same uncouth sounds.

Not many days since, hearing them busily engaged, we inquired what they were doing. They replied, "We have got a picture and are playing worship idols." Dark as midnight, indeed, would be our prospects in regard to the welfare of our dear children if the promises of God were not as many and as rich for us as for you, which after all, are the main springs of hope and

---

[91] Our children, from the age of 14 or 15 months, have been accustomed to sit still in their little chairs during our family devotions, and William Buck, since he was 19 months old, has attended church meetings regularly without making any disturbance. The baby we keep within hearing, as the exercises are held in a part of Mr. Goodell's house. The congregation the past year has been respectable, as to numbers and characters, for this place.

consolation. O for a strong and vigorous faith to seize hold of them and have our little ones now sealed the heirs of grace! Then could we contemplate with composure the storms of sorrow and temptation that may assail their path through the short journey of life and anticipate a happy meeting on the everlasting hills of light to exclaim before our Redeemer, "Here am I and the children Thou hast given me."[92]

It is one of the most interesting features in the character of maternal societies that mothers are educating their children not only for heaven, but for the church. This is the true character of heaven-born religion. This is a sure criterion that their zeal is genuine and has been kindled by the Spirit of God—that the plan will succeed till some mighty ends are accomplished.

Mothers, go on with redoubled energy and holy fervency of spirit! Your work is silent and unostentatious but takes hold of the destiny of future ages and of nations throughout the earth. Your daughter may hereafter be a solitary example of true female piety to multitudes in an unchristian or a heathen country. Educate her as much as possible to be everything that is amiable, worthy, and desirable as a wife. She may, at some future period, be the sole companion and helpmeet of a man of God under labors most weighty and trials most severe. Life, under God, in some solemn hour, may hang on her skill and tenderness to sooth.

Educate her in all respects for a mother. The first time she enters this solemn and tender relation, she may be far from her mother's guardian care; and perhaps may have no counsel and assistance to rely upon but her husband's. Multitudes of parents who never witnessed a pious family circle may look with wonder and profit at the manner she trains up her offspring and admire their sweetness of behavior and purity of conduct—or they may exclaim, "Her religion is no better than ours."

---

[92] Hebrews 2:13

Yes, your daughter, beloved Christian mother, if by your instruction, prayers, and example she be led to Jesus, she may preach a lecture on her dying bed that shall soften the hearts of the adamant and convert those to the belief and love of the gospel whom no power of argument could ever teach. Yea, it may be the means of a revival of religion in the darkest corner of the earth which shall be felt till the end of time!

My dear madam, I did not intend to intrude so long upon your patience when I began, but I hope you will forgive me. Do be so kind as to write us often, and freely impart such suggestions and counsels as your more mature knowledge and experience will dictate. We are ignorant (at least I am) and need to be taught. We want line upon line, precept upon precept.[93] And let us often be borne on your hearts to God.

I cannot close, however, without adding a line in testimony of the "Mother's Magazine." It is the first pamphlet we seize to read and value the most. It seems to me the editor's labors would not be in vain if it were printed for missionary mothers alone.

O, how happy must you be, dear friend, in seeing all your children the disciples of Christ! I know of no joy to a mother's heart equal to it this side heaven.

I thank you a thousand times for your present of books. They are worth more than silver or gold this side of the Atlantic. James Harrison and William come to sit in my lap every day and sing. William says, "Mamma, I will sing now; take the book." Mrs. Goodell and Mrs. Schaumer unite with me in Christian love to yourself and to those associations with which you are connected, to whose Christian sympathy we commend ourselves.

Yours truly,
Elizabeth B. Dwight

---

[93] Isaiah 28:13

Constantinople, Sept. 19, 1835

My dear Madam, [94]

The importance of your "circular letter" and the deep interest it excited in our bosoms would have called forth a much earlier reply had not sufficient reasons existed for delay. I have waited in order to report ourselves in the character of a Maternal Association, the formation of which has been retarded by sickness and various other obstacles. At length, through the goodness of God, we have met and adopted the articles of your constitution, as far as our circumstances would allow, resolving by Divine assistance under the solemn obligations such a maternal relation imposes, to attempt to more faithfully discharge the duties we owe our children, each other, the world, and our Redeemer. We number only three at this station—Mrs. Goodell, Mrs. Schauffler, and myself; but have added the names of Mrs. Schneider and Mrs. Powers at Broosa on our list, by their own request. They engage to observe the same time of our meeting for prayer; to remember each child often in their supplications, and to assist in maintaining a regular correspondence upon the subject of our maternal labors and obligations.

Thus our infant society embraces five members, and eleven children, and is doubtless the first of the kind ever established in Turkey. Certainly it is without a precedent in this grand metropolis that the Spirit of the Lord might bless our feeble beginning, and cause us in this, and in every other relation in life, to shine as lights in the midst of a crooked and perverse generation.[95] Inexperienced and alone as we are in a land of darkness, we do feel an almost overwhelming load of labor and responsibility resting upon our hands and hearts. We have long been aware, in some degree, of the influence and prosperity of

---

[94] Mrs. J. C , of Utica, N. Y.
[95] Philippians 2:15

the Maternal Association in Utica, NY, and now feel happy, in compliance with your kind invitation, to embrace this opportunity of appealing to your sympathy—to ask your counsel and your prayers for ourselves, our offspring, and the benighted parents and families among whom we live. That you do feel for the distant missionaries and their little ones, shut out from the privileges of a pure and refined society and the ordinances of the gospel in a Christian country, we have no doubt. You do weep and pray for us and contribute largely for our comfort. If however, instead of an imaginary picture, you could witness the reality of a heathen or unchristian society, I am sure your zeal would be increased, your prayers quickened, and your views of duty enlarged. But how shall my feeble pen attempt the representation? Oh think of millions without one clear beam of heavenly light to guide them in the path of holiness that alone leads to eternal life. The poor deluded mother knows no other way to heaven than through the daily routine of rote prayers and superstitious ceremonies; and how can she teach her children otherwise? All the spiritual light of the domestic dwelling is a taper kept burning before a picture of the Virgin Mary. To Mary the little one is taught to bow the knee and cross its breast in token of adoration while its heart is left a stranger to the commands of the gospel. The religion of this church is only a name, a form without life, a splendid shadow to dazzle the imagination and deceive the heart. Its oracles are dumb; and in vain does the mother lead her children there for instruction or consolation. Truth has expired in the lap of heresy, and an impenetrable cloud of superstition hangs over the altar of incense. The Sabbath returns only to be desecrated and is misused as an opportunity for the gratification of vain and selfish desires. On the Lord's Day, the mother, whose conduct should be allied to the employments of a better world, dresses her children out for a show, takes them to a temple decorated for fascination, and places them in the midst of a noisy crowd, who at certain intervals, bows down to the earth while a priest mutters an unintelligible jargon of nonsense. The remainder of the day is spent in folly and sin. The sound of the viol, the convivial throng in the ballroom, or the noisy mirth of the card table often disturb the tranquility of that hallowed eve, while the children are allowed to partake in the sins of their parents or are abandoned to the neglectful care of servants.

The frequent recurrence of "holy days" encourages idleness and pride, creates poverty with all its concomitant evils, and fosters self-righteousness in the heart. The rich seem to vie with each other, especially on these days, not only in decorating themselves, but also their infant offspring, with pieces of gold, ornaments of diamonds, and all the show of dress. The poorer class imitates them in the gaudy display of colors and other inferior appendages of show. A sweet little motherless girl used to exclaim on Saturday, "Tomorrow is Sunday—I shall wear my red silk frock!" Not many days since, we called at the house of a wealthy individual and saw a girl about six years old displaying a silver ornament on her head, set perhaps with sixty real diamonds, while she, doubtless, could not read a single word. Two small children, one nearly two years old, the other three, were carried about in the arms of servants to be amused and not infrequently did they exhibit the most perverse and obstinate disposition, which was encouraged by gratification. Another small boy within the circle of our acquaintance, left by Providence to the care of his mother, gained by her indulgence the complete mastery. He was dignified by a badge of office from the Sultan while in his cradle and was nourished to feel his importance which has already nearly ruined him. A while ago he leaped from the window of an upper story and nearly finished his existence. Would that these were solitary specimens of this kind of family government! If this is the way parents live and children are trained, do you wish to know how they die? Did one ever witness here a little sufferer triumphing over death and longing to burst its fetters of clay to go and praise the blessed Savior? No, all is gloom, darkness, and distraction in the chamber of dissolution. If death enters the windows and takes a darling child, the mother sits in sullen silence or raves with frantic madness. There is no Holy Spirit to come and sooth her wounded breast; no pious minister softly enters the dwelling of affliction and in accents of love points to the balm of Gilead and the physician there. The relatives gather flowers and roses and entwine a wreath to adorn the faded brow. They scatter golden tinsel over the lifeless form to be carried through the streets to its narrow home. Torches are lighted, and a priest is summoned to bear the cross, who is followed by a train of boys chanting the funeral service. Thus the dead are buried out of their sight and forgotten; and the awful warning is disregarded. I once saw a young woman, who died suddenly, carried by our windows arrayed in her accustomed habiliments as if for a party; and I involuntarily exclaimed, "Can this be death?"

O when will the dark night that now broods over the fairest portions of the earth be rolled away? Christian mothers, put this question to your heart and answer it. What have you done, what will you do, to usher in the daylight of knowledge and salvation and to awaken millions from the long sleep of ages? On whom does the redemption of our fellow creatures depend? Not upon the agency of angels, nor upon an individual of mighty energies, but on the Church of Christ united. The obscurest member cannot stand aloof from the work and be guiltless. The ransom price of a ruined world has been already paid by precious blood; and Christians, who have felt its saving, cleansing, power must make it known to the ends of the earth. Their lives, as well as their lips, must proclaim it. As well might we put up an effigy to represent a human being as to substitute the form for the substance of the gospel. The heathen want not only ministers of the Word, but pious, well-educated families in all the various departments of life to be the living, bright examples of the doctrines of Christianity. Then would the heaven-beaming countenances, the quiet deportment, the pure word of conversation, the upright, intelligent course of conduct, be so many arrows of conviction to wound the guilty breast. Then would the dwelling of domestic love, the altar of morning and evening sacrifice, the school-room of virtuous and religious knowledge, the Sabbath, and the sanctuary of public worship preach more powerfully than volumes of abstract teaching.

Beloved Christian mothers, here is room enough to scatter hundreds of your sons and daughters, who by bringing forth the sweet fruits of the Spirit, may make known, with unostentatious but irresistible power, the love of Christ and be the instruments through which God will save untold multitudes from endless perdition. Will you then train them wholly for God and give them up expressly to bear the glad tidings of salvation[96] to those who sit in darkness,[97] if He shall see fit to use them? Men of the world are ready to come, and do come, from all quarters of the earth for an increase of gold or honor; and shall Christians be less wise, or more backward, to serve the Master they profess to follow? Why is it that comparatively so few who love the dear Savior have been willing to leave their native land and become missionaries of the cross, unless it is because the thing has never been placed before them until their habits of life were fixed? Is it because early education, which inspired the love of home, had fastened a chain about them too strong to be broken by ordinary means? Methinks I hear you respond, dear sisters highly favored of the Lord, my children are His and I tell them so; and if they do not proclaim the message of redeeming grace where Zion sits in mourning, the fault shall not be mine.

O what a change would the balmy breath of heavenly life cast over this withered land! "The wilderness and solitary place would

---

[96] Isaiah 52:7
[97] Luke 1:79

be glad. The desert would rejoice and blossom as the rose."[98] "The mountains and the hills would break forth into singing, and all the trees of the field clap their hands. Instead of the thorn would come up the fir tree, and instead of the brier, the myrtle-tree."[99] Let us labor and faint not, and pray without ceasing.[100] The promises are sure—our work will soon be done; and while we are tuning our harps in heaven, may our dear children left behind be only separated from us by the narrow stream that divides eternity from time. Forgive me, dear Mrs. C., for this long, formal epistle; do write us with the greatest freedom and plainness, and permit us to profit by your rich experience. We feel daily our need of more wisdom and more grace. Could I enter your hallowed circle, I would cheerfully take the lowest place and rejoice to be a humble learner.

My husband and children enjoy good health; but mine is generally feeble. Dr. and Mrs. Grant, whom we love much, were at Trebizond preparing for their overland journey when we heard last. Our missionary work here generally prospers. Light and knowledge generally increase, and some souls are converted; but we want to see the heavens opened and the showers of grace descend until the whole land is watered. Please accept our kind and affectionate salutations, for yourself and family, and present them to your Maternal Society.

Yours in Christian love,
Elizabeth B. Dwight

---

[98] Isaiah 35:1
[99] Isaiah 55:12-13
[100] I Thessalonians 5:17

San Stefano, Sept. 19, 1835

Dear Mrs. Adser in Smyrna,

My heart responds to the sentiment "there is no place like home sweet home," especially to the fond wife and mother; and I hope you will find yours all that love, approved of heaven, can make it.

Disappointments, perplexities, and afflictions, however, are the lot of human nature, and perhaps they are the best portion of the Christian; these we must expect, and may they wean us from all we love most here below! There are temptations enough here on missionary ground to draw our hearts daily from God, as my experience can testify, though in America they talk about missionaries as if they had sundered every earthly tie and left all the world behind. How should I delight to see you personally and talk face to face on a hundred interesting subjects which we cannot discuss by pen.

I would kiss your sweet little James many times could he be put into my arms and wish him a thousand blessings far better than this empty world can bestow. May the Lord make him like Samuel of old—early His. I trust we shall sometimes pray for each other, as mothers, and for the little ones God has lent us.

We have just formed a Maternal Society with three members which we hope the Savior will bless for His own sake. It is high time our children were within the fold.

Dear Mrs. H. must have a world full of anxiety and labor with her own flock; and yet she has a school besides! I am afraid she will wear out too soon. The temptation is very strong to try one's strength to the utmost when we are surrounded by such multitudes of ignorant, deluded, and neglected children. I long to do something, and yet I am unable to do half my duty to my own family.

Affectionately yours,
Elizabeth B. Dwight

Sept. 20, 1835

Dear Susan,

I have had my heart full of congratulations for you and brother Schnieder since you have known the tender relation of parents. At the intelligence of such an event, memory returns immediately back to the period when I first became a mother, and then I can fully realize the mingled emotions of a mother's bosom at the sight of her firstborn babe; emotions too tender and solemn for any heart that has not felt them to conceive! May this cherished babe live to be the solace of its parents, if this is best. But should Infinite Wisdom otherwise order, it can never be lost from existence. Within that little infant body are enclosed, as you well know, immortal powers, which when unfolded can taste the joys of angels, if they are sanctified by the blood.

Could we who are parents, and could all who are not, be truly sensible of half the responsibility which our relation to our Creator and to our fellow creatures imposes upon us, we should sink beneath the amazing load. But alas! alas! how blind and thoughtless human nature is! How prone are Christians even to forget that all their enjoyments and afflictions and all their actions take hold on eternity!

Yours Affectionately,
Elizabeth B. Dwight

CHAPTER VI

Cords of Maternal Influence

Elizabeth's Concern for Her Children's Conversion

The following letter was published originally in the "Mother's Magazine" of December, 1836:

Constantinople, Pera, June 15, 1836

Dear Mrs. H.,

Your affectionate communication reached us a few days since and was received with feelings of the deepest gratitude by us all. It was just such a one as we greatly needed to quicken our slumbering energies and refresh our desponding spirits.

If Christian mothers in America will pray for us and our children, we must pray for ourselves and for them also. It is not in the nature of holy love—the love of Christian fellowship—to be passive; and if we have this principle in our hearts, it must be enlivened by such assurances as you have given us. It affords us incomparably more joy to know that our children have had one fervent prayer offered to heaven in their behalf than if treasures of gold had fallen to their inheritance; and we would humbly ask that they may not soon be forgotten in those hallowed circles where mothers in Israel meet to present their little ones to the Lord.

Since my previous letter, our maternal meetings have been continued once a fortnight, with occasional interruptions. We trust they have been productive of good to ourselves, in creating greater watchfulness over our own hearts, a deeper feeling of responsibility, a tender concern for our charge, and a more endearing bond of union between us.

Early in the winter, Mr. Goodell's eldest children were much more thoughtful and attentive to religious instruction than usual;

so that some special efforts were made to produce the conviction and conversion of all our number. I trust the Spirit of God was in some measure with us. It was proposed that we should all unite in praying on one day for one child, and the next day for another, till they all might be particularly carried to the throne of grace. We began on Monday with Mr. Goodell's eldest, and finished on Saturday with the youngest. The next Sabbath was appropriated to the children at Smyrna, the one at Trebizond, and the family of our Greek brother, Mr. Panayotes, by his own request. On the Monday following, Eliza Oscanian, and afterwards our children, were remembered; and on Friday, Ann Schauffler, and on Saturday, Susan Schneider. The plan proved such a source of comfort to us all, and produced such a sweet, fresh tie of Christian love, it has regularly been continued. Today is our own little William Buck's birthday. Though our families remain much as they were, and we see abundant cause for humility, we do feel an urgent necessity to go forward till our prayer shall be the prayer of faith that lays hold on the everlasting promises and saves the soul!

If we are warranted from the Scriptures to expect the early conversion of our children in connection with a faithful fulfillment of covenant vows—and who will dare, in this age of light, after all the pledges that have been given in answer to prayer, deny it—then how culpable are mothers in general! How much comfort do they deny themselves and their children! And, shall it be added, how many souls are ruined forever because they were not brought into the fold while under the influence of parental restraint and while within the reach of the means of grace!

"My children must be converted early in life" is a sentiment which ought to be adopted by every Christian mother and deserves to be written in letters of gold, daily before her eyes; or rather, so indelibly printed upon the heart, as never, for one hour, to be forgotten. And, happily, this is the feeling which is beginning to be cherished in our Maternal Societies. True, it must be accomplished through the grace of God, to quote your own language, "how freely bestowed!"

What sacred spot is there in our own country that is not beset with temptations at every step which threaten to destroy the youth, however virtuous? And if the pious mother at home could witness what we have often done in regard to her absent son in a foreign land, her soul would be filled with bitterness.

Dear sister, have you yet a child unconverted whom business, pleasure, or a thirst for gain or knowledge may call abroad beyond your circumspection or power of gaining information concerning his conduct, will you listen to a few facts by way of friendly warning? Shall I tell you of the young man who once knelt beside his mother in circles for prayer and who indulged a faint hope of having been renewed now profaning the Sabbath and afraid to meet a missionary, lest his ear catch a reproof?

Shall it be told that they who were faithfully nurtured in the precepts of the gospel break away from regard to moral obligations as soon as the restraints of society are removed; that their evenings are devoted to gambling and their Sabbaths to dissipation; that they scarcely or never enter the place where prayer is wont to be made? All this, and much more than this, is true. Alas! some have fallen in the midst of their days. Not far distant lies the moldering dust of fellow beings who in infancy breathed the New England atmosphere; and shall the sad tale be told to a weeping mother that her son died without hope and without God?[101] The Searcher of hearts knows whether the skirts of that mother's garments are free from the blood of her child. The Governor of the universe has done right.

Suffer me here to relate an incident in which we have taken deep interest. A young Christian lady from a distant country came here to teach the children of a brother. We called upon her

---

[101] Ephesians 2:12

when she first arrived and found her frank, amiable, and intelligent. Of her own accord, she introduced the subject of religion and stated the troubles of her new situation. She said she could not enjoy a quiet conscience without attending public worship on the Sabbath, as she had been accustomed to do; and moreover, she could not endure to witness card-playing and dancing on Sabbath evenings. "As well as I love dancing, I shall give it up, if I must dance on holy time, which the people here choose to do." Till that remark, we had secretly hoped she might be a Christian. However, after being here for several years, she met and married a native Catholic. Now we begin to shudder in view of her appalling danger. She said, "What would my father say if he knew I could fall into such temptations? I should never dare to see his face again. What would he say if he knew how my husband lived? I cannot grieve him by making it known. My mother is a good sort of a woman and is religious; but she is not like my father." What a declaration! A child in imminent danger of shipwreck, and yet no cord of maternal influence around her heart to restrain her in the path of safety! No secret act of faith in a mother's heart has linked the footsteps of her wandering daughter to the throne of God!

She continued, "Mr. F., the clerk of my husband, is the worst enemy I have to contend with. He importunes me perpetually to overcome my foolish notions. He says he is sure I shall join in the amusements, as heartily as the others, in three weeks, for he had the same reluctance at first, having imbibed these scruples from his parents." Oh had he been laid at the feet of Jesus early in life by a mother's wrestling intercessions, he might now have been instrumental of adding another soul to the company of the redeemed.

Months rolled away, and the young lady sometimes attended prayer meetings, though sometimes she was obliged to remain at home, but her mind was "like the troubled sea that cannot rest."[102] She had secretly imbibed some erroneous notions from reading the works of a certain noted author and was determined to stake her all upon their truth. She was prone to dispute and often came to our house with her favorite book to read passages for our benefit. At last the plague appeared, making awful ravages, and horror seized her mind. Infidelity or experimental religion was the alternative, she exclaimed. After a desperate struggle, the chain of self-dependence was broken and the captive sat, a willing captive, at the feet of Jesus! We "beheld the glorious change,"[103] and wondered and adored! Human authors were then cast away for the long-neglected Bible; and to the present period, she has adorned the Christian name and suffered, in her family, constant ridicule and persecution. She took the children to the church meetings, and commended them, as subjects of prayer, in our maternal meetings. She prayed with them and taught them to bend their knees before God. She has now returned to the arms of her earthly father, whose prayers have been answered under the most unfavorable circumstances. The child is redeemed! But will any reward come to an unfaithful mother? Is it not then of pressing importance that our children become pious in early life? Could a dying mother leave them here in peace while out of the ark of safety?

Can she see them rise to years of maturity and mingle in such a community without the grace of God? They must be converted, and blessed truth! All heaven is now willing to receive them there, and the pen of eternal love is ready to write the name of the youngest in the Lamb's book of life.[104] A brother lately remarked, in answer to the question, "How will our children hereafter be employed if they do not become pious?" that we had no right to make such a supposition—that we had given

---

[102] Isaiah 57:20
[103] II Corinthians 3:18
[104] Revelation 21:27

them to the Lord and ought always to feel and act in full assurance that they are His.

Should our children be left friendless and forlorn, we love to think there are friends in our native land who can feel the orphan's woes, and whom our heavenly Father would provide "to take them up;"[105] and should they need a portion of that knowledge which is the glory of our country, we would gladly, for a time, send them thither; but we need, greatly need, the assistance of pious children and youth *here*. There is abundant work for the children as well as the parents on missionary ground. They are wanted as examples of whatsoever is lovely,[106] to shine as stars in the midst of night.[107]

Affectionately yours,
Elizabeth B. Dwight

Aug. 28, 1836

Dear Mrs. H.,

In reference to your hardships, what do all these sorrows show us, but our own impotency and our daily need of lying as poor beggars at the mercy seat! But though we are poor and weak, our Savior is rich and infinitely kind. No good thing will He withhold from those who trust in Him.[108] What then have we to do when distressed with wants of any kind, but to draw near to Him for a heart to go—to look—to ask and live!

There is no fleeing from trouble but to flee to Christ—and O, when will our last sigh be hushed in His bosom! We shall not live, I fear, to see this wicked world transformed to a paradise, but let us do all we can to hasten its purification, that our children, and our children's children, may have a holier society

---

[105] Psalm 27:10
[106] Philippians 4:8
[107] Philippians 2:15
[108] Psalm 84:11

and a serener calm to enjoy during their earthly pilgrimage. If storms and persecution rage without and arrest every benevolent effort for the good of ruined multitudes, we dear sister have no excuse and I hope no disposition to remain inactive.

A world of care, labor, and responsibility devolves upon us as parents—as mothers who are to form the character of immortal beings. How large a portion of time do we need for mere reflection on such a subject! How much prayer is called for, and what moment can our hands and hearts be free, except when those dear objects of maternal solicitude are sweetly lost in slumber! Should we succeed by the blessing of God on faithful and unremitting diligence in training up our families for the kingdom of heaven, we should do much to aid the missionary cause by giving the world some lovely exhibitions of piety. But I trust the time has not yet come for us to feel ourselves entirely shut up at home in our opportunities of doing good. The Lord is nigh at hand,[109] though He may be behind a cloud.

Affectionately yours,
Elizabeth B. Dwight

Oct. 20, 1836

My dear Susan,

How weary I am is the language of my heart at the close of almost every day. What a tiresome world of toil and perplexity this is, and yet what have I done to benefit it or to prepare myself for a better world? It seems to me that I live only to fulfill an appointed period of time which is rapidly drawing to a close as day after day passes by; and yet it is certain we all do something more than exist. Every moment bears its report to heaven of good or evil. Ah, this awful alternative! If no good is done, sin is

---

[109] Philippians 4:5

committed! My heart is ever ready to escape from the bitter thought, but it profits not to hide our guilt from conscience.

We see enough and hear enough at the present time to stir us all up to fervent devotedness to Christ if outward circumstances alone could do it. Thousands are dying of the plague, every week, whose habitations we can almost see from our windows. They are vacated of fathers and mothers, of sisters and brothers, and of children, who are the hope and joy of their parents. The master and his slave find a narrow bed alike—cold, desolate, and lowly.

We witnessed a sight today that shocked me exceedingly, though I am told it is a very common one. In walking out this afternoon near the water, we discovered something resembling a human figure cast from a boat upon the wharf. It lay there for a moment perfectly unheeded. I asked my husband what it could be. He said it looked like a mummy, and so it did. It was wrapped in a piece of checkered cloth which was tied around the feet and breast. The truth soon glanced upon our minds. It could be nothing else than a dead body—from which the spirit had just been separated by the plague!

Presently a common porter took the stiffened clay upon his back, as if it had been an animal, and walked off with it towards the burying ground. It was the body of a Christian slave and was brought in the boat from the Constantinople side of the harbor. Slaves who remain Christians are always buried in this way and are not interred in graves but cast together into a large pit prepared for the purpose.

Our dear brother and sister Schauffler, and brother Smith, too—Oh, how deeply have they drunk of the cup of affliction! Who can heal so deep a wound but He who caused it or permitted it to be made? "Earth hath no sorrow that heaven cannot cure."[110] May each of them be assured of this in their own experience!

This is a lesson by which we ought to profit largely. We are united by the same tender ties, both of the conjugal and parental relation, and they too must sooner or later be sundered, though, for reasons unknown to us, ours still remain, while others equally tender are broken.

Affectionately yours,
Elizabeth B. Dwight

Dear sister Goodell,

Harrison's mamma is very grateful to sister Goodell and the children for so many birthday presents, whether Harrison is or not. Oh, if this could be his spiritual birthday! The words are often in my mind, "Thus far the Lord hath led me on."[111] Today, especially, have I been reminded of His goodness. Five years ago He carried me through my sorrows and never since has left me or mine to fall but has built up our household to a respectable number. O that every member of it might be trained up for the mansions above!

Harrison loves very much to hear the story about the marriage of the king's son and the man who had not on the wedding garment. Almost every night he wishes to have it repeated. I hope that he and William and Constantine will try to get the wedding garment, which is a clean heart, in order to go to heaven. Who can tell how soon the time may come when it will be necessary, and it ought to be always ready.

I thought of our maternal meeting, though I was alone; and tried to pray for your dear children as well as mine.

---

[110] From the hymn *Come Ye Disconsolate* by Thomas Moore
[111] From the hymn *Thus Far the Lord Hath Led Me On* by Isaac Watts

Yours affectionately,
Elizabeth B. Dwight

Constantinople, St. Stephano, June 26, 1835

Dear Miss P.,

Your favor of October 13, 1834, was forwarded last January, and also the valuable book which accompanied it, and were the means of exciting our gratitude and increasing our pleasure. It came by the hand of Mr. and Mrs Powers, who were the bearers of many such tokens of remembrance to our little missionary circle, and on seeing our joy, they remarked that they could not tell whether we welcomed them for their own sakes or for what they brought! We usually, after such a feast of intelligence, live in America for some days in imagination, tasting joys that flow sparingly, or not at all, in this barren land. Soon, however, scenes about us, and the calls of duty, bring home our wondering thoughts, and we feel again, with full force, all the wide difference of our situation. O that I could at once represent to your view the moral condition of Turkey as we behold it! The picture would be much more striking to you than it is even to us now, since we have been so long familiar with objects of degradation and misery and are absent from Christian society. Our residence in Pera was near the Greek Orthodox Church where we were often compelled to witness many appalling practices. Prayers are said in the church nearly every morning. The more superstitious or serious part of the people usually attend, though many of them never enter within the doors, but stand without at a little distance off and cross themselves at certain parts of the service. Several of the priests inhabit small rooms within the sacred enclosure and live in the most filthy and shameful manner. Their bloated faces and corpulent bodies, however, testify to their well-supplied tables.

They spend their time in apparent idleness and encourage others to do the same. The ceremonies at Easter (which came this year at the same time for all the different sects) were such as to make the true disciple mourn in bitterness of spirit and cease to wonder that the Turks think Islam is as good or better than Christianity. The mass, on that occasion, is always celebrated in the night, and no one thinks of retiring as usual. The beggars seat themselves beside the saint and keep up a continued strain of begging—the boys play and bawl aloud—loud guns are fired, and all is riot and confusion. One would be led to imagine it anything rather than the joy which a true believer feels on contemplating the resurrection morning of his Divine Savior. As soon as the service is finished, the first thought of every individual is to get something to eat, which has been denied through the long fast of forty days, and some even carry boiled eggs in their pockets to church. The sports are continued during three days, intermingled with processions and prayers. All business is stopped, and even the sedate Turk turns aside from his employment for recreation and amusement with Christians.

You can have no idea, my dear friend, what an anxiety it is to Christian parents in these countries to train up a family of children amidst such follies and wickedness—to hear them ask, what means this, and why is that, and at the same time to have no churches to lead them to but such as are polluted with idolatry. There is something wonderfully imposing to the young beholder in massive buildings glittering within with gold, and silver, blazing lights, and figures of saints, and in gaudy processions of priests and bishops. This looks something more like religious worship to the unrenewed heart than the humble meeting of a few individuals at a private house. Yet it is as easy for the Spirit of God to guide the infant heart in the ways of holiness here as anywhere, and for our consolation He has bid us to trust Him with all our concerns. It is only the want of active faith that ever leads us to indulge in distressing fears.

Our dear sister, Mrs. Schauffler, has been very low of late, beyond the hopes and expectations of all her friends. The prospect of her recovery is now more favorable. She has a young son about six weeks old. Mrs. Goodell has a babe two months old, and our youngest is seven months. My health is very feeble.

Your letter left Miss E. in a sad state of health. I wish to hear again her state. Many I knew and loved at home could be found no more should we return now. The constant experience of mortality among our acquaintances, and especially among the little band of missionaries, ought to rouse up every energy of our souls to "live for Christ."[112] Two from Syria have passed into glory within the last year.

Sabbath eve, 28th. I have been shut up this day to my own reflections, unable to go out. Harrison preached at Commodore Porter's to seven hearers. I have been trying to fix my thoughts on a better world and praying to be ready for it. Very soon all our earthly Sabbaths will be at an end. We may never spend one again in the same temple here below! Shall we, dear sister, meet in the kingdom of our Father above? Pray ever that we may— and do not forget our dear children. It is hard to think of our leaving them behind in this wicked world, unconverted. And it would be still more so to see any of them die strangers to God. O! there is an abundance of salvation for us and all our friends. Let us believe, and we shall be satisfied. Harrison unites with me in the kindest regards to yourself and your honored mother. I beg a kind remembrance to any friends who may take the interest to inquire for us. Do write as often as possible.

Yours in constant friendship,
Elizabeth B. Dwight.

---

[112] Philippians 1:21

CHAPTER VII

Evangelizing Little Ones

Elizabeth's Letters to Her Nieces

Constantinople, Pera, Dec. 4, 1835

My dear little Niece,

Your mamma tells me your name is Cornelia and often writes something about you, so that I feel acquainted with you, though we have never seen each other. I often think of you and want to see you very much and to know how much you have learned since you have lived in this world. I sometimes forget how old you are. Can you read? Do you go to church and love to learn whatever is good? Do you always obey papa and mamma and love them very dearly? I suppose you are too small yet to write, but as soon as you can, you must write Aunt Elizabeth and tell her all about yourself. Mamma has often doubtless told you about your little cousins here in this far off place, James Harrison, William Buck, and baby John White. William is about your age, yet I think bigger and fatter, and he is very fond of play. I wish you could have been here today, for it is Johnny's birthday. He is now one year old, and God has been very kind to take care of him and keep him from harm. If he were old enough to talk and know about his Creator and Preserver it would be right for him to pray and thank Him with all his heart and ask the forgiveness of all his sins, but as he is now too young to understand these subjects, his papa and mamma have tried to thank God for him and to give him up to Jesus Christ, who loves little children and died to save their souls from hell. Although Johnny is so young, he has a wicked heart, and so have all other children, which if they ever go to heaven, they must first be washed clean in the blood of Christ. Yesterday Johnny was picking up some bad thing from the floor (as he often does, to put into his mouth) but he saw his papa come in and look at him, and then he dropped it down, for he knew it was naughty and so wished to deceive his papa. Do you not think it is quite wrong for a little child to do a thing when his parents are out of sight which they forbid? Did you, my dear, ever try to deceive? I hope not—it is very sinful, and no sin is small in the sight of God.

Now I will tell you what we did today. I invited Mrs. Goodell's five children—Eliza, Abigail, William, Constantine, and Isabella—to come and spend the afternoon and take tea with us. Little William Samuel Schauffler was asked also, and as he could not come, I will copy the note his papa wrote in reply for him, that you may know what he says. He sent with the note a red box with some sugar-plums in it and a small book for a present for Johnny. It reads:

Dear John,

I rejoice with you that you have safely arrived at the venerable age of twelve months. I can't remember your birthday, but I suppose you can, and I will take your word for it that it was a year ago. I should have come over today to manifest my sympathies by jumping a little with you, but your kind note was miscarried. At present I am about to "turn in" as the sailors say, and you may perhaps be already in your cradle or bed, but I thought I would send you a line and wish you many happy years in this world [a rare privilege] and a happy eternity hereafter. I believe my mamma will contrive a present for you. I don't know what it may prove to be, but such as it is, I beg you to accept of it kindly and believe me your very affectionate fellow traveler to eternity.

Signed, William Samuel Schauffler

I don't know if you will understand this note, but mamma will tell you what it means, and I will tell you how happy all the young friends were together. They all ran and jumped about the room and laughed when no one could tell what the matter was, and sometimes forgot that little John was much smaller and feebler and would tumble him over in their glee. Then his mamma would have to come and take him up and sooth him for a while. Mr. Goodell said they must all return home before dark, so we had tea early. Mr. Goodell left a good old gentleman, Mr. Panayotes, to take care of them, because Mrs. Goodell was sick and he was obliged to stay with her. We had some bread and butter (which we do not always get), some stewed sauce of apricots, and some kelvar, a thing you have never seen in New-York. Mr. Oscanian can tell you what it is. It is very sweet. The children ate of it heartily and were as happy as they could be. Your uncle Harrison asked the children who they thought was the wisest person at the party. They said "Eliza Oscanian, because she is the oldest," for they think she belongs to the young party. Uncle Harrison told them the oldest were not always the wisest, and that some people who know a great deal are yet foolish because they are wicked, and that wicked people are always foolish. And now, do you think little Cornelia is wise? If she has given her heart to the Savior she is—if not, you are a wicked and foolish girl. It is wicked to live one day without loving Christ after we are old enough to know about Him.

Do you ever go and ride with papa and mamma in a chaise or coach? There are no chaises or coaches in Constantinople, but instead of them the people use arabas, usually drawn by a pair of oxen and sometimes by a horse. I think you would be ashamed to be seen riding in one of them in New York. The other day we got one, and I took William Buck to ride out with me and see a friend.

Please give Aunt Elizabeth's compliments to Mr. Oscanian when he comes to see you, and tell him he must be your amanuensis to write me a letter, and inform me all about your little self if mamma cannot find the time. Please give my love to papa and mamma and all the dear friends in your house, and accept much from your aunt and uncle and little cousins in Constantinople.

Your affectionate aunt,
Elizabeth B. Dwight.

Constantinople, Pera, Oct. 12, 1836

My dear little Niece Cornelia,

Your dear mamma says you are very fond of hearing stories, and if I can write anything that will amuse and profit you (for I wish to do both) I shall be happy. It is sometimes difficult to realize what we do not see, and I want to give you some sensible token that you have friends who think of you, love you, and pray for you, though they live far off beyond the wide seas and the great Atlantic Ocean which washes the shores of America.

Now and then one of those fine ships which you see living in the harbor of New York spreads its noble sails to the wind and comes here, and once your papa sent Harrison a whip and some books. At another time Aunt Delia sent the children a little dog and a horse-cart and grand-mamma some cake. Then they knew for certain that they had many good friends somewhere! The dog and cart stand on the bureau in our parlor now, but the whip has been worn out.

It takes a vessel about two months to come from New York or Boston to Constantinople, and if you will ask mamma to show you, you can find the way on the map. After the passenger in the ship has bid adieu to dear friends and set sail, he first loses sight of the houses, then catches a farewell glance of the steeples which tower above them, till at last the land looks only like a distant cloud, and it is no more seen, and nothing but sky and water for many weeks surround him. The little weary land-birds can no longer accompany him but fly homewards toward the shore.

A little girl would think it very dismal to be long shut up in such a watery prison and would exult for joy to see again the green earth. I remember when we first reached land, I thought I would never be unthankful for any comfort in a quiet house again, however poor it might be, I was so tired of the rocking sea. But our hearts are very deceitful, and I soon forgot this good resolution and have since received many blessings from God without praising Him.

Then we had to set sail again from Malta to Constantinople. It is delightful to sail in fair weather among the islands in the Grecian Archipelago. The week before we passed through the Archipelago, a number of pirates went on board an American ship and took the captain's watch, money, knives, and forks, and all his furniture, and a large quantity of coffee. We thought the Lord was very good to let us pass in safety.

When the wind blows hard, the angry waves dash with fury against the rocks and roll up beyond their usual limits on the shore, as if they would destroy every thing within their reach. The boatmen draw their slender barks high on the sand and are afraid to venture out in them. Do you know who stills the waves and the tempests, and says, "Thus far shalt thou come and no farther"?[113] Do you know who once walked on the water and did not sink, and who once said to the wind, "Be still,"[114] and it ceased? You will say it was Jesus. It is He, too, that has prevented wind and water, thunder and lightning, the hand of cruelty or sickness, from causing our death, and how should we love Him!

A great many young men spend their Sabbaths here in shooting for amusement, and in the evening of these precious days, they drink and smoke and sing and play so loud as to

[113] Job 38:11
[114] Mark 4:39

disturb the whole neighborhood. Do you not think this is very wicked? It certainly is, and God will one day severely punish those who dishonor the Sabbath if they do not repent and turn to Him. The people of this place are poor, ignorant, and superstitious. Most of them are Greeks. They live in unkept houses and spend much of their time in idleness, loitering about their doors. The men are principally occupied in fishing and rowing boats, and they might make their families much more comfortable if they did not spend what they earn during the day at the wine-shops in the evening. After the harvest, the hungry children are sent into the field to glean the heads of the wheat, as Ruth of whom you read in the Bible gleaned the field of Boaz. We often saw two poor women turning round a large heavy stone wheel placed upon the top of another to bruise the wheat placed between them. They said it was to make pilaf, because they were not able to buy rice.

St. Stefano was named by the Greeks in honor of the first Christian martyr, Stephen, who they suppose watches over that place. Once a year they keep a feast-day for him, which is spent in idleness and sin. We read of such a good man who was stoned to death, and received up to heaven, but we do not know that he takes care of any particular place, and besides we are to worship God only.[115] There is a church also dedicated to St. Stephen, which has a picture of the Virgin Mary and the cross of Jesus Christ to which the people bow down instead of loving and serving Christ as the Bible commands. One of the priests used to keep a school in it to teach the children a few prayers and some other things in a language they do not understand called Latin. A kind-hearted man saw how pitiable their condition was, and got them a good teacher, and fitted up their room with seats and benches, and provided them with books and slates. For a while the parents were pleased, and the children learned well. But the

---

[115] Luke 4:8

old teacher, who wanted to get the money, said the school was his and made much trouble about it—so it was all destroyed, and the poor boys and girls were left to run again about the streets.

I want to tell you of how two little children died there of the plague once. Their father was a boatman and brought the plague in his clothes or something else from the city, for no one in the village was sick. The little girls died after suffering a few hours pain, and the people were afraid to go near the house. The father took one in his arms and carried it to the grave, and then he returned and conveyed the other to the same spot. Then he and his wife were together alone and knew not what to do or where to go for comfort. They had no more children—they knew not the promises of religion—their friends were afraid to approach them, and they were driven from the house to a miserable tent to smoke themselves and their clothes for some time. Oh how we grieved and pitied them, to see these young people laid in the dust before they had been taught the way to heaven. There are many more now, as ignorant as they were, who may die at any time—and will you pray God to send them instruction and prepare them for a better world? The parents here are not like your papa and mamma. They believe foolish lies instead of the truth.

Do you remember how I copied a letter for you that William Samuel Schauffler sent to John White on his first birthday? That dear boy is now cold in death, and his little brother about two months old sleeps quietly by his side in the grave. The name of the other was James Ferdinand. We think these two dear babes are with Jesus Christ, praising Him, and are much happier than they could be in this world of pain and sorrow. Their parents were very much grieved to lose both of their sweet children at once, but they had given them to the Lord who made them and believed He has done right.[116] They rejoice to think that they

---

[116] Genesis 18:25

have become like angels, free from sin, and that they are wearing crowns of gold, tuning harps of heavenly music that God has given them to enjoy forever. Should you not love to be their companion and even be willing to do without papa and mamma for a while to be a happy saint above the sky? Then pray to be holy—to be like the dear Savior, "who carries the lambs in His arms and gathers them in His bosom."[117] This is a verse that William Buck loves to repeat, and how I wish that you, Cornelia, and he, may be some of those dear lambs. No matter then when your body dies; the spirit will live in glory, and at the resurrection a new shining body will be formed out of the sleeping dust, for Jesus says it shall be raised again. The wicked too will be raised but only for everlasting shame and misery.

James Harrison turned six years old last Sunday. Some friends gave him many little presents which I fear he thought more about than he did of thanking his heavenly Father who has kept him alive so long. All our little boys would be very glad to see you and their other cousins. They have only six playmates here, and now we have to live shut up in a house almost like prisoners, because the plague, a terrible disease, is causing many people to die.

Now I have told you the way to Constantinople, and you can learn the names of the great ocean, and the seas and the straits between us, if they are not too long and hard. Mamma will tell you the difference between an ocean and sea, and what a strait is, and an island, and a cape. I am sure little William Buck cannot tell, but I suppose the children improve faster in America than they do here. William has read a part of Mr. Gallaudet's primer with Isabella Goodell, which your dear mamma sent. He loves to read about Frank and Jane and how they went to church. Have you got a book like it? When you come and see me, you may sit in the balcony with Harrison, William, and John, and look out of

---

[117] Isaiah 40:11

102

the window and see the different sorts of people pass. There are many nations here—Turks, Greeks, Jews, Armenians, French, English, Russians, Italians, and Arabic. We live in the main street of Pera. Perhaps I shall send you a little curl of my hair, and some of William's, which is now straight, that you may see the color, and then if you will send me some of yours, I will keep it in a paper carefully with cousin Elizabeth's and Delia White's. Love to your papa and mamma.

I am your affectionate aunt,
Elizabeth B. Dwight

Constantinople, Pera, Sept. 22, 1833
My dear nieces Elizabeth and Delia,

I received a few lines from each of you last spring which were very acceptable, and which would have been acknowledged long ago had not so many other things occupied my time. And now, my dear Elizabeth, you must forgive me if I seem to address you as the little girl you were four years ago instead of the young lady which your letter indicates you have become. I hope you both will hereafter write us many letters, for if your papa and mamma write every month as they propose, still we shall not hear half as much as we wish to know. As your letter is not now at hand, I have nearly forgotten what you wrote about except the amusing affair which happened at the commencement of lighting the meeting house for the evening exercises and the little stories Delia so prettily related.

We have taken an Armenian girl who is about twelve years old to educate. Her name is Eliza Hoskins. The females in this part of the world, both young and old, do not improve their time as they do in our beloved country. They sit at the window from morning till night gazing at any passing stranger. A poor ignorant girl sits at the door of her cabin near our house every day, with a gold chain about her neck without any sort of productivity.

The plague has lately broken out again in some places here; a dreadful disease such as you have never heard of in America. Scarcely an individual has it and recovers. A few days ago we saw our neighbors hanging out a long line of wool garments, handling them carefully with iron rods and not touching them at all with their hands. Upon making inquiry we learned that a servant in their house had just been seized with the plague and carried away. I hope this calamity will not spread, but if it does, we must be content to let the Lord's will be done. We are always exposed to death in every place, whether we are old or young, and the only way to live happy and to lose the fear of death is to fear God and put our trust in Him through Jesus Christ, for He will always do what is best for those who love Him and confide in His mercy.

I owe your dear mamma a letter or letters and a great many other friends besides, and I hope they will not cast me off for my negligence. When I have learned how better to redeem time I will better do my duty.

Your uncle has now rung the bell for prayers, and I must obey the summons and bid you good night. James Harrison and baby have long been hugging their sweet pillows. I told James Harrison that I was going to write his cousins, and he said mamma might send his love to you, too. We send much love to your papa and mamma, and Aunt Susan, and yourselves.

Your affectionate aunt,
Elizabeth B. Dwight

Constantinople, Sept. 26, 1835

My dear Sister Cornelia,

I owe you not only a letter, but a great deal more which I cannot repay, and people are apt to think when they get to be bankrupts and cannot pay the whole, they may as well pay nothing. I cannot, however, feel quite satisfied to let the present opportunity pass without saying a few words to thank you, which my heart does a thousand times, for all your accumulated favors. The night after the arrival of so many letters and packages by Dr. and Mrs. Grant, we scarcely slept at all from the excitement they occasioned, and it was not till long afterwards that we regained our usual state of mind. At that time my health was very miserable, and I was getting low spirited, and you cannot imagine how much those precious books from Mrs. H. awakened my desires afresh to live for the sake of my dear children.

The "Nursery Songs" and "Mother's Hymn Book" are an invaluable treasure, and I would not consent to part with them for any price. James Harrison sings some of the tunes very prettily, and William Buck imitates with good success, and now and then breaks out alone even in company, "O, if I were a robin, I would fly away!" What will become of our little ones is a question that arises in our hearts daily and causes no little solicitude. I sometimes feel myself a burden on thousands of others, instead of doing anything to help forward the cause of Jesus Christ. I think I should be content to be removed out of the way, yet when the wants of our dear children are realized and seen, life appears important and doubly precious. For who can fill a mother's place to her offspring if she at all does her duty in this land of unfeeling hearts? What servant will smooth the babe's pillow and hush its heart to rest when mamma is sick, or who will tell the older ones a Scripture story and lead their minds to Jesus when papa has not time to perform a double duty? Happy for us, the "hairs of our head are all numbered."[118] Our minutest sorrows we may tell the blessed Savior, and the humblest request He will not despise. We shall be spared on earth as long as He has anything for us to do to help lead the precious lambs that He has redeemed with His own blood into His bosom.

---

[118] Matthew 10:30

How I should love to see your sweet little Cornelia and witness the bestowment of your fond care. Children now advance forward so fast in America that soon she will be able to write aunty a letter. I began to write her some stories last spring, but they appeared so foolish compared with what mamma could tell her they were never sent. How highly favored you are, dear sister, in being able to attend such enlightened Maternal Societies. In return for such privileges, you must remember to "do good and communicate,"[119] and try to benefit your sister. I have just written Mrs. Hastings a long letter which I was almost afraid to send when it was finished. You must derive a great deal of pleasure from the pleasant and profitable society of that family; would that we could participate with you one week at least. We have lived very retired this summer and almost without Frank society, there being only one family (Com. Porter's) in the village who speak English, and it is so quiet being alone, that I almost dread returning to Pera, which we shall immediately be compelled to do. It is truly pleasant to be out of the gaze of the fashionable world when we have no necessary communion with it.

The plague has been in the city, too, from which we have been comparatively in no danger. As quiet as we live now, Harrison has had scarcely an hour to study for the last two weeks from the calls of company. If he had not good health and patience, too, he would soon be worn out in body and mind. Why cannot you persuade brother W. to rest a year and take a voyage with yourself and little Cornelia here to cheer us up and strengthen our hands? I was going to tell you when I began the letter how apropos little Johnny's frocks came, and he felt quite proud too that little coz had worn them first. They fitted exactly, and were the very articles his mamma would have been obliged immediately to make. I almost fear I shall feel proud in wearing

---

[119] Hebrews 13:16

that beautiful silk from your hand, especially as Mrs. Grant said you had a similar one when she saw you. Dr. and Mrs. Grant were at Trebizond the 11th, troubled in procuring horses for their journey. They hoped to leave soon. Eliza Oscanian sends her love; she is a very bright girl and speaks English with as much ease as her brother did when he left. She has made a good deal of improvement since she came to us in almost every respect, yet there is room for a good deal more; above all we want to see her truly pious.

I hope, dear sister, you have regained your health since your last letter. It is painful at such a distance off to hear our friends are ill, as it is a long time before our suspense is relieved. Do take all possible care of yourself. I do pity dear sister Susan, but if her trials are only sanctified they will be better than worldly consolations. What bright prospects in her case have been blasted!

Harrison preached at Com. Porter's today to eight hearers, not much like Mr. P's full assembly. With much love to brother and to your household,

I am your affectionate sister,
Elizabeth B. Dwight

CHAPTER VIII

He Does all Things Well

Elizabeth's Last Letters

Constantinople, Pera, Jan. 29, 1837

My dear Sister,

Time slips away so rapidly! I cannot tell when I wrote you last, but conclude that it is some months since. At any rate, my pen has lain almost inactive since we came back to the city, and many other desirable things, as well as writing, have been neglected for the want of assistance in our kitchen.

Our former servant has now again returned, being satisfied with her experiments of change, as well as we, and I hope she will be induced to rest quiet; otherwise, the burden of nursing, and domestic cares too, may come upon my dear husband, who has enough of his own already. I assure you, he has now some gray hairs, which perhaps he may not like to have spoken of, for he only acknowledges that his wife is wearing out and growing older! Next Friday will be my birthday, and if you will come to celebrate it, we will kill the fatted Turkey! Otherwise, it will probably pass unnoticed. Last Thursday was appointed as a day of special thanksgiving in our missionary circle in order to recall some of the ten thousand mercies we all have experienced since our residence in these lands and that a spirit of more fervent gratitude might be awakened in our hearts.

It is no small testimony of the distinguishing love of our Heavenly Father that none of our families has been smitten by the pestilence while so many thousands have fallen around.[120] It is as true as trite a saying, "that one half of the world does not know how the other half lives." Misery and sorrow, dear sister,

---

[120] Psalm 91:6, 7

you have scarcely seen in New England. Had I time and room, and you patience to read, I could tell you many a tale of distress. The past autumn has been one of no ordinary affliction in this city, and yet where is there an individual that will pause to inquire "wherefore has the Lord smitten us"?[121]

I think I have not written since the many articles you purchased for our comfort came, and I now thank you much for your trouble. Alas for the poor ball! The net makes James Harrison a good purse to please him, but William took a pin and tried the ball to see what effect a puncture would have upon it! I suppose he did it because he was expressly told it would spoil it. As for the shoes, they are a treasure we shall not return, while there are so many little feet here of all sizes, but only two pair are large enough for James Harrison, so we may trouble you the sooner again. Mine fit well, and especially the ones you had worn; they are exactly the thing, and I had the pleasure of wearing them for the first time to church meeting on Christmas day. So far from being offended at receiving what you had previously used, I wish I could tread in your shoes oftener—I do not mean literally however! Mrs. Goodell and I have been shopping today to obtain things for friends in Persia and Broosa.

I remain, with love to all, your affectionate sister,
Elizabeth B. Dwight.

The extract which follows is from a letter addressed to a female friend, then resident at Malta, where it will be recollected Elizabeth spent more than two years of her missionary life. The letter was written after a long period of close quarantine on account of the plague.

---

[121] I Samuel 4:3

Dear Mrs. Temple,

Malta appears to have many attractions now, since having been shut up so long in this place without society and without being employed in any direct labor for the evangelization of the inhabitants. Though you breathe so many lamentations of uselessness, I feel happy in the thought that you and Mrs. H are so well employed and are exerting an influence in so many ways.

Yet surely there is enough on all sides to discourage any one of us in these dark regions, without a strong and lively confidence in that Divine Power, which often causes the sun to shine forth from under the darkest cloud. But I trust it is the Lord who has directed each of us to the stations we now occupy, and it is our duty and happiness to do with all our might whatsoever our hands find to do[122]—leaving the event with Him.

Your affectionately,
Elizabeth B. Dwight

The following was written soon after she gave birth to her fourth child and about three months previous to her decease. It was addressed to a beloved missionary sister in Broosa, Mrs. Susan Schneider.

My dear Susan,

My thoughts and affections towards you have not been so inactive as my pen for some time past. Nor could they be, for every now and then some kind token comes from you to awaken them afresh. Patience—patience, what a word! and care too; they have a world of emphasis and meaning. I need much more of the former, and wish others, with whom we have to deal in our families, had more of the latter. But you will think this strange talk for one who has just been the recipient of so great mercies.

---

[122] Ecclesiastes 9:10

And true enough, gratitude is a more becoming and proper subject for my words and thoughts. Before I was expecting it, a song of deliverance was put into my mouth.[123] Although I had taken special care for some weeks to avoid getting cold, yet the day before my confinement,[124] a severe influenza came on which produced a constant headache, cough, and all the other accompaniments of such a disease. I dreaded the consequences, but the Lord was infinitely gracious in the hour of peril.

We do indeed love our new baby boy enough, and I would not raise my hand to have him what he is not, for the Lord knows how to suit His gifts. Perhaps, should we all live a few years longer, we may tell him or some of the older ones to go to Broosa, Trebizond, or somewhere else among our friends of a kindred spirit and bring us a daughter to comfort us in our old age. Ah! old age! Who of us missionaries may expect to reach it? Infirmities we may feel, but threescore years and ten, though at the pace time flies it might soon seem to come—who of us will see that period completed? Who of us can wish it? Is it not better to have our work done and go home the earlier to be at rest?

Yours affectionately,
Elizabeth B. Dwight

The two letters which follow were the last letters Elizabeth ever wrote. The one to Mrs. Susan Schneider was written late in the evening previous to the breaking out of her disease and while she was suffering from a headache, which was, in fact, a premonitory symptom. The other, addressed to Mrs. Powers, was written two days beforehand. Mr. and Mrs. Powers, in consideration of her debilitated state, had very kindly offered to help care for her two eldest boys; and this note, as will be seen,

---

[123] Psalm 32:7
[124] i.e., time of labor and childbirth

contains an allusion to this proposition. Those two boys have since been placed in the family of these dear missionaries at Broosa—although when the offer was made no one imagined that they would so soon be left motherless.

San Stefano, June 25, 1837

My dear Mrs. Powers,

I am not unconscious how much I am in your debt, neither am I ungrateful, although it might appear so. All your notes, labors, and kind offers are duly appreciated and serve to remind me constantly how valuable and pleasant it is to have good sisters, though they may be hundreds of miles distant. If all the followers of Christ were as ready to do all the kind offices they might, even near at hand, many a heart would sing for joy that now aches for the want of sympathy and tender care.

I did not dream that you would volunteer to burden yourself with our children to relieve me; though I should have had no doubt but your kind heart would have answered "yes" had we requested it. I should feel sorry to be obliged to lie so much upon you and trust we shall not at present burden you in this way, yet I feel as thankful to you and Mr. Powers both, as if you had already received them. Mrs. Schauffler has much care to manage with so large a family, which it grieves me not to be able to relieve.

My health and strength are somewhat improved, and could I get over one difficulty that obliges me to remain quiet, I could perform the customary duties of my family as formerly. And it is from the inability to do this, and not from anything that I suffer, that I find myself becoming impatient; for my condition is one of mercies and comforts only. Yet even in this I sin.

The Lord, our tender-hearted, merciful Savior, would not inflict the slightest pain or evil upon any of His people which He did not see necessary for their best good.

113

There are two families almost by our own doors in quarantine who are far less comfortable than we. A child belonging to one of them died last week with some sores which made them suspect it was the plague. They were out of doors the next night in a storm without a tent. We gave them some sheets and such things as we could, and the next morning, some dry clothes for the baby. Such deprivations in sickness we know nothing about, and when they come to our knowledge, they serve to shame me for ever having indulged a complaining thought.

How painfully affecting is Mr. and Mrs. Adger's affliction! My heart bleeds for them whenever they come into remembrance, and yet how sweet to see Christians, in such circumstances, mourning with true godly submission—there is so much of the spirit of heaven exhibited! Mr. Adger's letter to Mr. Schauffler when their last babe died was very touching, and Mr. Schauffler's so much so in return, that I begged a copy to be sent in the name of our Maternal Society to the Mother's Magazine.

I hope you will get more and more strength this summer and be prepared both in body and spirit to see the descent of the Holy Spirit upon the poor perishing souls in Broosa—a blessing which we hope may be in store and which we all so much need here. Without His power, no plant of grace will spring up or thrive in the human heart in any clime.

Your affectionate friend and sister, with the kindest regards to your husband,

Elizabeth B. Dwight

My dear Sister Susan,

It seems to be my fortune to receive instead of conferring favors so that my debt of gratitude has become a large one to you and many others.

I sometimes grieve that I can do nothing to repay it, though perhaps there is some pride as well as gratitude mingled with this feeling. It is humbling to human nature to be always dependent, and this is a lesson that I need to receive no less than many others. But besides this, it draws the human family much nearer together, and this is a compensation worth suffering for.

The more I am cast upon the tender mercy of friends, the more I value their worth and am drawn towards them. It is, however, a painful thought to consider one's self a burden on the hands of others—especially upon the labors of those who have the unsearchable riches of Christ to make known to their fellow men.[125]

But we are to walk by faith—not by sight[126]—with the confident assurance that our Father does all things well; and what more can children wish? How glad should I be to visit you this summer! I did hope, last winter, that it might be so, and that the trip might take the place of a removal to the country, yet it is ordered otherwise. I should be glad if my husband could rest for a while and refresh himself with you during the summer, yet I need him so much that I feel hardly willing to relinquish him until I have more strength.

I do really seem to myself, and doubtless to others also, childish. When I had strength, I thought myself something, but now I shrink before a straw in the wind. The doctor has ordered frequent sea-bathing, which I intend to try.

---

[125] Ephesians 3:8
[126] II Corinthians 5:7

Little Johnny suffers this summer again from the bowel complaint and often looks much emaciated after several days of severe diarrhea. We do not remain without anxiety for him, and his mother can most tenderly sympathize in all his weaknesses and self-denials.

With what fondness have we watched for his progress in talking this whole year, and yet "papa" and "mamma" are the only words he can articulate—nor does he know the name of a single object, while his apprehension by signs is very acute.

With much love to all, I am most truly yours,
Elizabeth B. Dwight.

&

CHAPTER IX

The Consolations of the Gospel

Elizabeth Enters Into Glory

It was probably very far from Elizabeth's thoughts that when she penned that letter to Susan, it would be the last she would ever write; and yet the very next day she was laid upon a bed of sickness from which she never rose! So it will be with us who survive. We shall soon, perhaps unconsciously, write our last letter, make our last prayer, speak our last word, and spend our last day and our last hour upon the earth!

Happy will it be for us, if like her, we have put our house in readiness, so that we can never be taken by surprise. But miserable beyond all account will be our condition if when the stern summons of death comes, we have not yet begun to make our preparation for eternity.

Death—to the unregenerate sinner—is awful! But it has no terror for the Christian! The Christian should make death and eternity his familiar study. He should regard death not with gloomy forebodings as too many who bear the Christian name are wont to do—but with the most eager and joyful anticipations; not as something to be avoided but to be coveted. Death to the Christian is that which separates him forever from sin and unites him forever to Christ! Is it not, then, an object to call forth his earnest desires? It terminates all his anxious and hazardous conflicts with corruption and introduces him into a dwelling-place of perfect and unchanging purity! Is it not this for which he has been longing and striving all his life? And shall he shrink from such a deliverance—from such a consummation of his best hopes and wishes—from such untold, unimagined glory?

The great difficulty in the way of our taking the most cheerful and encouraging views of death is the extreme weakness of our faith. If we had faith as a grain of mustard-seed,[127] we might easily remove these mountains of doubts and difficulties and cast them into the sea of oblivion. With the most free and explicit promises within our hands, we hesitate to lay hold of the full privileges of the Christian hope, and we tremblingly shrink away from a complete reliance on the cross of Christ.

The gospel ground is the cross alone, and to that, and to that only, is the sinner directed to look and live. To whatever other quarter he turns his eyes, it is all "the blackness of darkness;"[128] but there is nothing but pure unclouded light. "There is no condemnation to them that are in Christ Jesus, who walk not after the flesh, but after the Spirit."[129]

We cannot fail to notice how carefully guarded this is against Antinomian abuse; while at the same time it gives to all who struggle against sin and trust in the cross of Christ the fullest warrant to hope joyfully. "It is God that justifieth, who is he that condemneth?"[130] Truly! and it may be asked, if God can get over the difficulties in the way of our salvation, what need have we to be harassed any more on account of them? If God has found out a way by which He is willing to justify us, shall we, in doubt of His sincerity or ability, condemn ourselves?

If we have sins great and aggravated, Jesus Christ has merits reaching far above them all. To doubt this is a species of infidelity highly dishonorable to God. All that is needed of us is simple trust in Christ. The hope that arises from such confidence, however, is a purifying hope. If sin—external or internal—is loved, cherished, and habitually practiced, it shows that we do not trust in Christ as one who came to redeem us from all iniquity,[131] for we do not desire such a redemption. But

---

[127] Matthew 17:20
[128] Jude 1:13
[129] Romans 8:1
[130] Romans 8:33
[131] Titus 2:14

if sin is our burden, if it causes us daily anxiety and trouble, we have not even the slightest ground to doubt when we look to Christ. He is able to save to the uttermost them that come unto God by Him.[132]

Let us lift up our believing, joyful hearts to Him, and then death, even in the most horrid form, will be welcome. The agony will be short and it will terminate gloriously!

It is always gratifying to know what are the feelings and experience of a Christian on his dying bed with all the solemnities of eternity fully before his mind.

In Elizabeth's case, as we have seen, her disease was such as to deprive us, in a great measure, of this gratification. Her mind was evidently weakened by it almost from the very beginning, and soon after, she lost the power of utterance and lay for the most part in a state of stupor. Sometimes, however, she seemed to be roused from this stupor, and would probably have talked rationally, had she not been deprived of speech.

At these times her husband had some conversations with her; she replying by signs, as she was requested. The following extracts are from a journal kept by him at the time, and they are inserted here with the belief that they will be read with interest in connection with what has now been communicated:

"July 3—It is a great grief to me that, in my present trying situation, I cannot talk with my dear wife of the love of Christ; of His presence and all-sufficiency, and of His precious promises, and often pray with her in reference to our going to meet Him in another world, for I feel that I may go with her, and perhaps before her. She lies in a constant state of stupor and can hardly be roused to take a spoonful of arrow-root or a little medicine. She cannot listen long to what I say, or to my prayers, for she easily falls asleep, and even when she does listen, she cannot tell

---

132 Hebrews 7:25

me her feelings, for she has no power of utterance. Just now, observing that she appeared more roused than usual, I put to her several questions, requesting her to answer me by a motion of the hand.

"I inquired first about her pains of body and then asked her if she would like to have me pray with her; to which she replied, by a sign in the affirmative. I asked her, "Are you happy now, my dear?" She gave the affirmative sign. "Do you feel that Christ is very near and precious to you?" She made the affirmative sign with great promptness. After repeating some passages of Scripture, I prayed, and when I arose, I was pleased to see that she had been enabled to give her attention throughout. I then selected a portion of Scripture to read, but she could attend no longer, for she had fallen asleep.

"Elizabeth has just opened her eyes for a short time. I asked her if she had comfort of mind. She made no motion and perhaps did not understand me, as her hearing is evidently affected. I asked her again if on this sick bed she could trust her all in the hands of Christ. She made the affirmative sign with the greatest promptness. I then repeated to her these two precious assurances of Scripture, 'I am the resurrection and the life. He that believeth on Me, though he were dead, yet shall he live.'[133] 'For our light affliction, which is but for a moment, worketh out for us a far more exceeding and eternal weight of glory.'[134] She soon closed her eyes again in sleep."

"July 4—My wife does not sleep so much today as usual, and she is rather restless. I saw her just now lying with her eyes open and asked her if she could adopt the language of Paul, and say, 'I know whom I have believed and am persuaded He is able to keep that which I have committed unto Him against that day.'[135] After a moment of deep thoughtfulness, she made the

---

[133] John 11:25
[134] II Corinthians 4:17
[135] II Timothy 1:12

affirmative sign. I then told her that a few days of suffering here will never once be thought of when we are tuning our hearts to the praises of our Redeemer in heaven. Afterwards, I kneeled down and prayed by her bedside. When I arose, I asked her if she understood the words of the prayer, and she made the negative sign. I supposed it arose from a difficulty in hearing."

In conclusion, we may be permitted to make a few suggestions to Christians at large, who may read these pages. And in the first place we would say: let all who have hearts to pray cry mightily to God in behalf of missionaries. We know not through what fiery trials they are passing while we are living at our ease. At any rate, from their very situation they are exposed to troubles more than other men and need the special grace of God. They go out with the expectation that their lives will be shortened by their peculiar exposures. Pray that their faith and Christian courage may endure to the end, and that their labors, though short, may be abundantly productive.

Again, pray for the children of the missionaries. Their exposures to temptations are many and great. If they are not early converted, there is great reason to fear that they will fall into some disgraceful sin. Christ would thus be wounded in the house of His friends.[136] Besides this, they are often left orphans or deprived of a father or mother. Where in America is the Christian father, or the Christian mother, whose heart is not peculiarly tender and affectionate towards the children of departed missionaries?

Third, let none be discouraged when valuable missionaries are taken away. Do you think if the Lord needed them in order to carry on His work that He would remove them? They are sometimes called away suddenly from very useful labors, and we are apt to feel that there is a serious loss sustained; but, although

---

[136] Zechariah 13:6

many have been thus called away, the missionary work has suffered no arrest in consequence, but on the contrary, it has steadily advanced. Nay, if we could ascertain the truth, we should doubtless find that in most cases, these very removals of dear missionary laborers from the field have been the means of far more abundant good than if they had remained. Their surviving fellow-workers have been rendered more faithful; eternal things have become more familiar; the world and its lying vanities have been more effectually excluded; prayer has become more fervent and importunate; the miseries of perishing souls have taken a deeper hold of the heart; and more energy, point, and purpose have been given to every labor of their hands, because they have felt that the time is short. In this way, by the grace of God, great blessings have come out of sore afflictions.

Finally, one great thing that is needed at home and abroad at the present day, and that is closet-religion [i.e., prayer].[137] If we have this, we shall never place such dependence upon instruments as to be disheartened or disconcerted when these instruments are removed. If we have this without borrowing any trouble from the future, we have the best preparation possible for trials and afflictions. An active bustling piety, merely, is not suited to the hour of fiery trial any more than it is to the calm and solemn stillness of the dying bed. Nor will the Lord accept of even the fullest stretch of bodily and mental activity in His service as a substitute for self-mortification, subdued passions, and a spiritual and heavenly mind.

All that religious activity abroad, which is purchased at the sacrifice of closet-duties, is delusion to the soul and a mockery in the sight of God. He wants the heart—the whole heart; and without this, even duties of His own appointment become abomination in His sight. No man can have true spiritual life without keeping his heart with all diligence, for out of it are the

---

[137] i.e., prayer. See Matthew 6:6

issues of life.[138] And no man can keep his heart with all diligence who has not an in-door as well as an out-door religion; and who has not a closet for prayer and meditation as well as a world for bustle and action.

Ah! is not this a point of deep deficiency with many of us? Must we not acknowledge with shame that while we have been laboriously cultivating the vineyard of the Lord, and endeavoring to make it appear beautiful without, we have suffered rank weeds to take root and spring up in our own hearts? To our closets then let us go, and may we meet the Lord there daily! When we have once shut the door, let us never open it again to go out to the world until we have felt the powers of the world to come, have had sweet believing views of Christ, and have been refreshed by some precious foretastes of heavenly glory.

෨

---

[138] Proverbs 4:23

19970603R00073

Made in the USA
Middletown, DE
10 May 2015